Puffin Cove

Table of Contents

For Betty, who dreamed of and prepared for a life of sea adventures, and our sons, George and Gene, who helped us enjoy them.

1

Discovering the Lonely Islands

We wanted a simple life. Many young people dream of such a life but find it slipping from their grasp as college or vocational training and then work and family responsibilities take control of their lives. Unlike most maturing couples, we didn't outgrow our dreams of a small seaside cabin where we would take our food from the sea or land instead of buying it at a supermarket.

I joined the U.S. Navy in 1940, going from a farm in Michigan to a battleship in the Pacific Ocean. Betty was raised on Fidalgo Island in Puget Sound. She often talked about her childhood, especially the happy summers she spent with her family on various islands in the sound near her father's salmon traps. After college in Southern California, Betty knew she wanted to live in the Pacific Northwest. We were married just after Pearl Harbor, and our sons, George and Gene, were born during World War II.

We held on to our dreams through World War II and the Korean War.

After many moves up and down the West Coast, we knew that California, Oregon, and Washington were too crowded for us. Betty wanted to live on one of British Columbia's bays or inlets. She had become enamored of British Columbia one summer when she rowed her Indian dugout canoe from Puget Sound to Southeastern Alaska—alone. I wanted to go to Alaska, where I would have veterans' rights for homesteading. We agreed on two things: moving north, and getting out of the navy.

In 1953, at the end of the Korean War and after over thirteen years of service, I resigned my commission. We now had time, monthly mortgage payments on two houses—both rented—and no income.

In 1954 we set out in *Thunderbird,* a nineteen-foot Grand Banks codfish dory, to search for a homesite on Vancouver Island. By day we cruised along the coast, fished, or hiked the lonely beaches. At night we camped ashore. After ninety-one days, we returned to Anacortes, Washington. "Vancouver Island is too civilized," I told my in-laws.

Then, the following spring, we headed for the Queen Charlotte Islands. Comprising some 150 islands and islets, they are the peaks of a submerged mountain chain, 156 miles long and one-third as wide. Located about sixty miles from the mainland coast, these are Canada's westernmost islands, and, on a clear day, one can look across Dixon Entrance and see the snow-covered peaks of Dall and Prince of Wales islands, Alaska.

We spent the spring and summer exploring the islands. Black bears freely roamed the beaches. After the first few days, we could almost ignore the deer, which had been introduced for hunting. There was a year-round open season on both sexes, but they had no natural enemies. As a result, the deer had rapidly increased and could be seen munching kelp or sleeping in the sun on nearly every beach.

As we cruised the Charlottes' waterways, we could hear

the various cries of bald eagles, gulls, ravens, oyster catchers, loons, and peregrine falcons. Seals popped up alongside the boat to stare at us. River otters preened on tidal rocks, and marten loped along drift logs. Bald eagles wheeled on out-stretched wings above us, and salmon leaped and splashed in the water. Besides salmon, trout, halibut, and lingcod abound-ed; ducks and geese were plentiful; and clams and abalone could be dug or picked at low tide. We were in a Garden of Eden.

Around us, the land was covered with dense rain forest, mainly western red cedar, Sitka spruce, western hemlock, and yellow cedar. Dead gray snags protruded from the virgin forest. Stumps, tops, and limbs covered newly logged areas. An even height of light green trees healed the scars of land logged fifteen to twenty years earlier—trees to be harvested at the turn of the twenty-first century.

Approximately twenty-five hundred persons were scat-tered around the Charlottes in six permanent villages and three logging camps—fewer than the crew of the 888-foot aircraft carrier I had served on in Korea. This was a small community where almost everyone knew each other.

Traveling around Moresby Island, we explored the ruins of numerous Haida villages. At Anthony Island, on the remote southwest corner of the Charlottes, we visited the sunny, silent village of Ninstints, which has the world's largest collection of standing Haida totem poles—more than two dozen. Although the one-hundred-year-old poles were gray and cracked, their features were still sharp and the boldness and symmetry of the designs still apparent. Some leaned precariously; others, toppled by age and gales, lay rotting on the damp soil, splotched with moss and lichens.

The carved-out receptacles of mortuary poles were empty, their cover planks gone. Salal and berry bushes grew from cracks and crevices in the soft wood.

The village also contained excavations of over a dozen

longhouses. The mortised corner posts and tenoned cross braces of two stood upright and higher than my head. A low cliff rose behind the longhouses, sheltering the village from west and north winds.

Some of these communal buildings had been about thirty by sixty feet. The entrance was a low, narrow opening. Only one person could enter at a time, leaning over, so it was easy to hit an enemy on the head.

Sleeping shelves were cut below ground level all the way around the interior. Children played and adults worked, talked, and cooked food in the large central portion. Smoke escaped through adjustable openings in the gable roof.

It is unknown when the Haidas came to the Queen Charlottes or where they came from. Around the time that the first European explorers arrived, some of these Indians migrated across Dixon Entrance and settled on the southern tips of Dall and Prince of Wales islands. The largest settlement there is Kaigani, a name often used to identify this land.

European explorers recorded that generally the Haidas were not much darker than Europeans. On average, they were about five feet, seven inches tall, large boned, thickset, and muscular. Dark eyes and black hair were usual, though a few had hair described as chestnut-colored.

The village was the largest political entity, and villages were often rivals. Within a village there were three classes of chiefs: the town chief, family chiefs, and house chiefs. Family chiefs had the right to refuse to participate in any offensive battles planned by the town chief.

Society was matrilineal; inheritance was through the mother's line. At an early age sons were sent to live with and be taught by a maternal uncle, whose crests, positions, and wealth these nephews would eventually inherit.

Women wore lip plugs for ornamentation. At puberty, a small bone pin was inserted into a girl's lower lip. As she grew, the pin was replaced by ever-larger oval wooden disks, until, at maturity, a labret 2½ inches wide and inlaid with abalone shell weighed down her lower lip, exposing the teeth.

Both sexes wore ornaments of abalone shell or silver suspended from the septum and pendants of copper, shell, or animal teeth suspended from the ears. Young men and women were tattooed on the breast, back, shins, and forearms; in addition, men were tattooed on the thighs.

Slaves, either captured or purchased, were a measure of an individual's wealth. Their treatment varied from reasonable to cruel. Years later, the venerable hereditary chief of Chaatl, Solomon Wilson, told us, "My father's slaves were always given blankets, allowed to fish for their own needs, and given freedom to travel—within the islands." He left us with the impression that slaves were treated as poor but respected members of the family.

Occasionally wood with iron, copper, or bronze fittings drifted ashore. From these rare finds, the Haidas fashioned knives or chisels, using slate or sandstone to keep them sharp. With the coming of the white man, tools and utensils became readily available. During the early years of trading, a sea otter pelt might be exchanged for a small, inexpensive iron hand adz.

The Haidas made large and exceptionally seaworthy canoes from western red cedar. This light, straight-grained wood is easily worked and slow to rot. The largest dugouts were about seventy-five feet long with a beam of seven feet and were capable of transporting three dozen paddlers and two tons of cargo. Most canoes were smaller—twenty to twenty-five feet long—and powered by one or two persons.

Eventually the white man's diseases greatly reduced the Haida population, forcing the survivors to abandon their ancestral homes and move to the villages of Old Masset (now Haida) and Skidegate Mission, where they could obtain medical attention, trade for supplies, and build smaller homes heated by the white man's stove.

With the coming of spring, Haidas continued to depart their villages, canoeing off to family campsites to fish and hunt. The women tended small gardens and gathered the eggs of wild birds, vying for the large eggs of sea gulls. Berry picking and fish and herb drying added to their summer activities. Even today most Haida families continue the spring rite of netting sockeye salmon and preserving it for the coming winter.

Today many Haidas work as fishermen or loggers. Just as the white man's stove replaced the central fire pit, his boats and cars have now replaced the handsome dugout canoe.

On August first we headed up the west coast of Graham Island, beating into northwest seas, and then along the north shore to Masset. We had weeks without an hour of sunshine— nothing but mist, fog, low clouds, and rain. For the first time in our lives we had boils. Scratches and cuts festered instead of quickly healing.

Much of Graham Island is low. We decided this region of flat land didn't appeal to us. We liked the wild, rugged west coast of Moresby and Kunghit islands, where we had felt the sunshine.

The question was, when could we afford to quit work and leave the smog, crowds, and bumper-to-bumper traffic of Southern California?

2

Starting in Sandspit

When we returned from our trip to the Queen Charlottes, I enrolled in a two-year course at Brooks Institute of Photography. At the end of the course I got a job supervising the processing of motion picture film at the U.S. Naval Missile Center in Point Mugu, California. In the meantime, Betty was teaching disturbed children at Camarillo State Hospital.

The years passed. We kept our dream of paying off our debts and moving to a secluded waterfront home, but at times it seemed we were moving away from our dream instead of toward it.

Finally, in April 1964, while I was struggling with our income tax, the trigger was pulled. Forms and papers covered the kitchen table and overflowed onto the floor: statements and receipts for property tax, sales tax, gasoline tax, excise tax, federal and state income tax, and a few lesser taxes. These figures told me we were working every year from January first until sometime in April just to pay taxes.

"We're being penalized for working!" I screamed, pounding the table.

Each year these taxes were increasing, demanding a larger percentage of our income—more of our time and more of our lives.

"There's more to living than working three or four months every year just to pay taxes!" I growled at Betty. "Especially when we don't have the satisfaction of truthfully saying, 'Federal, state, and county officials, we're pleased with the way you carefully husband and conscientiously use each of our tax dollars. We're proud to have a small share in every one of your well-thought-out, beneficial, and useful local, national, and international programs.'"

Those tax figures and unbridled government waste cost the nation, state, and county two hard-working taxpayers.

I added together our assets. We owned our home and heated swimming pool on two oceanfront lots in Ventura County. I had a 115-acre farm in Michigan—where the federal government *paid* me not to raise crops. And each of us had at least a million dollars' worth of strength and good health.

At forty-two I was fast approaching my top earning years. But was a regular paycheck and four pensions all we wanted out of life?

By doing without many of the things we were used to—two or three cars (never enough for four licensed drivers); magazines and newspapers; book club and record club selections; dining out; concert and theater tickets; short vacations and meaningless trips, none giving real satisfaction and rest—we might be able to stretch out our assets until I reached age sixty, when I would receive a pension for naval service during two wars and in the reserve. There was always the possibility of getting a part-time or seasonal job as well.

We would try a financially insecure but free life.

In 1963 we had leased land at an unnamed lagoon we called Puffin Cove and at splendid Gilbert Bay. I was determined not to move to a foreign country without owning property, however, so we bought an oceanfront lot in Sandspit, only a half-mile from the airport.

In May 1964 Betty flew to Anacortes to help her brother Bill convert a twenty-six-foot metal-hulled lifeboat into a boat we could use to get around the islands.

"It should last a year or two. Just long enough for us to find something better," Betty wrote. (We are still using it in 1982.)

By June the boat was ready, fueled, and provisioned. I arrived in Anacortes one day, and we departed for Sandspit the next, entering Canada as "Summer Settlers." With us were tools for construction and a few household effects. We enjoyed an easy trip up the picturesque Inside Passage and across smooth Hecate Strait to Sandspit.

George and his wife, Mary, and Gene and his girl friend, Sherry, flew in to help build a small house. Betty had ordered a precut sixteen-by-twenty-four-foot one-bedroom cedar cabin.

At that time the coastal freighter *Skeena Prince* departed Vancouver every second week for the Charlottes. I phoned the mill manager and notified him of the ship's schedule and of our own limited time. "Don't worry. Your cabin will be aboard." he told me.

His words reminded me of that other well-known phrase of reassurance: "You can't miss it!" Somehow I usually did.

Our lot, once the site of a small sawmill, was littered with rejected logs, slabs, broken machinery, and a rank growth of salmonberry bushes. One large, bent spruce stood near the back. Two or three small trees reached above the bushes. We cleared and burned, and then dug a trench for the concrete foundation.

We had found two of the survey stakes—the two alongside the main road. I assumed the lot was perpendicular to the road, but I felt uneasy. Finally I obtained a plot map, and with the boat compass and a long tape measure we found the elusive stakes. Our lot was plotted at an angle to the main road. "We'd have built on a proposed future roadway!" I barked when we found the fourth stake.

When the *Skeena Prince* arrived, the cabin material was not aboard. The mill manager leaped to number one spot on my list of incompetents. This was also the beginning of my disillusionment with being a distant customer.

I returned to California. Already I had had a two-week extension on my month's leave.

Betty, George, Gene, Mary, and Sherry poured the concrete foundation. Two weeks later the cabin material arrived. They erected the cabin in one day. It went together like Lincoln Logs and looked like a dressed-up log cabin.

The young people returned to college—after Mary delivered our first grandchild, a boy, in Oregon. We had hoped he would be born in Canada and have the benefits of dual citizenship.

Betty was left to do the best she could about water, electricity, and a septic system. She hired the airport electrician to moonlight installing the wiring, while she crawled around underneath the house pulling or pushing wires. During the day she dug the pit and drainage field and built a septic tank. In her spare time she dug the well through sand and clamshells, making cribbing as she worked down to fresh water at seventeen feet. For recreation Betty squeezed in a couple of dugout canoe trips through Skidegate Narrows to the west coast.

In the meantime I sold our beachfront house to a Hollywood doctor. Then I sold, gave away, or dumped nearly everything we had accumulated in twenty-three years of marriage. The only things I kept were books, photographic materials, tools, hunting and fishing gear, clothing, and my navy uniforms. Not much for a middle-aged couple to start out with.

In June and July of 1965 I completed my tour of duty as

executive officer of a harbor defense unit, took my annual two weeks of active-duty training aboard a new Landing Ship Tank, and submitted my resignation as a civilian employee of the Naval Missile Center. At last we were free to start a new and totally different life.

Driving north to join Betty, I listened to the news on the radio: another murder-suicide in Los Angeles, a gang rape in Watts, and a seismologist's prediction of a destructive earthquake along the San Andreas Fault. None of the five million persons within range of the station really needed to be informed by the weatherman that the weekend would be dry, sunny, and warm, and that the inversion layer would continue to hold the Los Angeles basin under stinging, choking smog.

I was leaving all this. Leaving the crime, the violence, and the smog, but also the security of a well-paying and interesting position, California's salubrious climate, and an oceanfront home with heated pool. All that for a small, isolated cabin on the edge of a rain-forested island in the stormy North Pacific. Was I crazy? Some acquaintances in both California and the Queen Charlottes thought so.

I picked Gene up in Anacortes. We drove to Vancouver, put the pickup on the *Skeena Prince,* and flew to Sandspit. Upon arriving, I inspected Betty's job of construction. The doghouse-sized shelter she had knocked together from scraps to protect the water pump didn't rate effusive praise. But the well and septic tank system did.

Two problems immediately beset us. First, the cabin was too small for three of us. The living room couch might be comfortable enough for Gene, but he really needed a room of his own. Second, the well had gone dry.

Water took priority. Gene put on his hip boots and slid down a rope to the bottom of the twenty-foot length of thirty-six-inch galvanized culvert pipe standing inside the well's cribbing. He shoveled wet sand into buckets, and I hoisted and dumped them. As Gene undermined the pipe, I jiggled it down.

Soon the pipe was down another three feet and chill water splashed above Gene's knees. And this, old-timers assured us, was a dry summer.

Having taken some courses in architecture at college, Gene offered to draw up plans for the house. Lofts could be made at each end for sleeping. A photographic darkroom would fit nicely behind the angled, off-center fireplace. Another bathroom could be put in one corner. Windows should fill the south side, and a row of skylights would provide adequate light even during short winter days.

Construction might have been faster if we had ordered all materials from mainland building suppliers. Instead we salvaged or beachcombed everything we could find, and the rest was shipped in. We now had more time than money, so we did all the work ourselves. Besides, there were few people around to hire.

That first winter in the Charlottes surprised us. Although we knew that the *Kuroshio* (Japan Current) modified the climate, we were amazed by week after week of mild weather—just like Puget Sound and coastal Oregon. Of course there were many days of rain or drizzle and one or two violent downpours. There were also a few snowstorms. Afterwards snow clung to trees and wires and lay in thick blankets on rooftops for a few days.

The main difference was wind—days of wind, including a few tree-toppling hurricanes. Our small, electric-heated cabin was snug, sheltered from southeasters by acres of tall, second-growth timber.

Betty, Gene, and I worked nearly every day on the addition. On rainy days we often drove to an old quarry and selected a load or two of rocks for the wall or fireplace.

Cutting cedar shake bolts in the burned-over area around Skidegate Lake was satisfying but dirty work. The timber had been felled and bucked in the midfifties. Then a fire swept through, and the charred logs were left to rot. As a result, we had to go through a layer of blackened wood to get to the dry, straight-grained shake material. Some of the shakes made from those logs were eighteen inches wide. Emil Larka, a Finnish friend who is a superb outdoorsman, taught me how to make shakes. His own small house is roofed with shakes a foot wide and over twelve feet long.

The addition, which is larger than the original cabin, took nearly a year to complete. One long wall is made of rock. We built a large fireplace with the hearth a comfortable sitting height above the living room's brick floor, where sparks and embers land without danger. An extra-large door, made of two-inch-by-six-inch planking, allows us to bring in a small boat for repairs or roll in a wheelbarrow full of wood to feed the voracious fireplace.

Today nearly two dozen large Japanese glass fishing floats hang from open rafters in the living room. The ten-foot lower jaw of a sperm whale stands alongside the fireplace. Nearby, a fourteen-inch-high and nineteen-inch-wide vertebra from a sulfur-bottom whale serves as a stool. The fireplace mantel is a beachcombed Japanese hatch board made of Port Orford cedar—grown in Japan—decorated with bronze dolphins—insignia of the submarine service.

Overloaded bookshelves line most walls. Any other space is occupied by enlarged color or black and white photographs, silk-screen prints, and souvenirs of our years in the Charlottes.

There is a chart table in one corner of the room, and above it is a compartmentalized shelf filled with rolled charts of the Pacific. *Thunderbird's* nameplate, the only part of the yacht salvaged from Betty's shipwreck in 1940, is nailed to one of the crossbeams.

Our home isn't much like other houses, but it suits our needs and we like it.

3

April around Moresby Island

Skylark, our twenty-six-foot converted lifeboat, spent that first winter in our yard. We pulled out the Oldsmobile straight-six engine with its hydromatic drive (virtually no power in reverse; sometimes I stopped by crashing into something) and installed a new Volvo-Penta marine diesel. The gas engine burned three gallons an hour; the diesel, less than half a gallon. Now we wouldn't worry about blowing up every time we lit *Skylark's* wood stove.

April was frequently a month of sun and calm, according to the old-timers. We hoped so, because the D-8 Cat brought out of the bush and into Crown-Zellerbach's camp was available to launch *Skylark* in the bay in front of our house. After a landlocked winter, we were anxious to get underway.

"You sure won't see a launching like this at any marina," I told Betty as the Cat dragged our metal boat over sprouting grass, across a gravel road, down a steep embankment, and onto the dry tidal flats. *Skylark* rode on a grid of two short poles lashed to a pair of cedar logs about twenty feet long.

A fresh coat of chrome yellow sparkled on *Skylark's* galvanized hull. The decks had been painted battleship gray. The sides of the cabin were white; the top, an easy-to-see international orange. A still-tacky coat of protective copper paint covered *Skylark's* bottom, and new line and galvanized chain were bent to the thirty-five-pound Danforth anchor. The 110-gallon tank was topped off.

Our double sleeping bag was on the wide forward bunk. Gene had claimed the upper bunk to starboard, where a porthole let in light for reading. Bags of clothes and supplies filled the lower bunk, and the shelves behind the fold-down table were packed with food. The water tank was filled; we would cut firewood for the stove along the way. The stern compartment was empty—waiting to be jammed with beach-combings. We were ready for a month or more of wandering through the Queen Charlottes

Shortly after noon, *Skylark* was bouncing gently as slight incoming waves began to lift her. I climbed aboard, ready to start up and give the engine a test run.

We were afloat. The engine started instantly, and cooling water soon flowed from the overboard discharge.

I threw the drive into forward and we were underway. "This is great!" I said to myself, smiling with pride and satisfaction.

But why were we moving so slowly? The anchor wasn't down and dragging. What had I done wrong? Maybe the engine was too small.

I looked over the side to get a better idea of our speed—or lack of it. "You idiot!" I yelled at myself.

Skylark was still on the grid, trying to shove a six-foot-wide path through the water. I tried reversing suddenly. Then full throttle ahead. Nothing—that grid stayed with us. The Cat was still on the beach. I drove the boat and grid hard ashore and, feeling foolish, went looking for the loggers.

The Catskinner laughed. "No problem," he said, probably figuring I was as dumb as the mongrel running up and down the beach chasing sea gulls. He started up the Cat, snapped a short butt onto the gravel, drove into the water until the hydraulic blade was against *Skylark's* bow, and then lowered it across the logs, pushing them under water. *Skylark* was free.

"You were right, Neil," Betty said when I picked her up at the wharf. "I've never seen a launching like that anywhere!"

Billowing clouds drifted with the northwest breeze as we crossed the long spit separating Shingle Bay from Hecate Strait and turned south. The rippled turquoise water sparkled with a million tiny mirrors.

Second-growth timber covered the shore and the low, rolling hillsides until we neared Gray Point. From there to Cumshewa Head, the uninhabited coast was covered with virgin timber.

We anchored at Skedans, on Louise Island. I was pleased with the new diesel. It pushed us along at the same speed as the guzzling Olds.

From *Skylark's* decks we saw at least a dozen totem poles, some tall and straight, a few leaning at drunken angles, others toppled over. Rough boulders rose like giant steps along the eastern promontory, and weathered rocks and a reef lay to the west.

Sitka and Ivan, our Samoyeds, leaped into the dugout as soon as Gene launched it. A seal popped up to have a look at us.

Ashore we found other totem poles hidden among the trees. These weathered gray carvings were rapidly deteriorating. Two standing poles we had photographed in 1955 were now rotting in the moist ground.

"Look here!" Gene called. "Three skulls!"

Three human skulls, one jawless, lurked in the grass. The teeth were in excellent condition, testimony of the Haida's healthful diet. (Bones lay exposed at many of the old villages, and we still see skeletons in unfrequented places.)

After a lingering look, we climbed over the jumbled pile of drift logs ringing the upswept beach where dugouts up to seventy-five feet in length once beached, stepped into Betty's fourteen-foot dugout, and rowed to *Skylark*.

Our next stop was Cumshewa Village. Entering Cumshewa Inlet, we passed the site of an old trading post at McCoy Cove. At the village, two aged mortuary poles stood like silent watchmen on a green clearing, where a gravid doe was browsing.

It was cool in the forest. Many of the totem poles had been pushed aside or split by growing trees, and shrubs or small trees sprouted from others. Gnarled crabapple trees and clumps of nettles and thistles covered a clearing that was probably once used to grow potatoes and tobacco. Only a thin trickle ran through the abandoned village's single creek—and this was spring.

We crossed the inlet back to Louise Island and went up Mathers Creek to the site of another Haida village, New Clew, which had been established in 1887 by survivors of the smallpox epidemic at Tanu. There were no totem poles here. Death had trailed these Haidas. Graves were marked with marble stones bearing inscriptions that reflected the influence of missionaries during these deadly years—for example, "Kitty Kitsawa, she was a Methodist," and "He tried to be a Christian." After ten years the survivors of New Clew moved on to Skidegate Mission.

During the war massive Sitka spruce were taken from this broad valley drained by Mathers Creek and used for aircraft construction. The trees cleared to make the passage were sawn down the center, laid on pilings, and cross-braced at the open center; then the outer edge was rimmed with small log halves. Miles of this gently curving, gradually rising log road ran into the island's interior to Mathers Lake. British Leyland trucks with hard rubber tires had run along the wooden tracks like a train; there was even a turntable for reversing the empty trucks.

Sixteen wrecked trucks sat in the campsite clearing at the seaward end of the roadway. Tumbled frame buildings littered the area. Discarded caulked boots, tools, enamel cookware, cast-iron stoves, wire rope, crosscut saws, axes with broken handles, and, of course, broken bottles defiled this otherwise lovely spot.

In a half-hour of fishing at Mathers Creek we landed enough cutthroat trout and Dolly Varden for our evening meal. Though it was midafternoon, the bright spring sun guaranteed at least another four hours of daylight. We motored up the inlet. To port, a wooden water tank loomed above the broad clearing behind Beattie Anchorage, site of another derelict logging camp. To starboard, numerous buildings and a network of pilings marked Aero, the Charlottes' only railroad logging camp. Beyond, at the inlet's head, was Moresby Camp.

"Things sure change fast around here," I said. "In less than ten years Aero has been abandoned and Moresby Camp opened."

We turned south, through narrowing Carmichael Passage and into Louise Narrows. The tide was ebbing as we skimmed over the gravel bottom, bouncing once in the S-shaped, bulldozed channel as I watched a large bear stroll along the shore. "It's the first one I've seen this year," was my excuse.

A pelagic cormorant staggered into the air from its perch on a drifting deadhead. From an overhanging branch a belted kingfisher dove into the clear water, flying off with a tiny, wriggling fish.

We anchored in Lagoon Inlet. In the tidal water and on shore were the ruins of a salmon cannery. The sun gradually lowered behind steep mountains; the temperature dropped quickly. Ashore, Betty searched among the ruins for small opium bottles cast away by Chinese laborers.

"Gene and I will pick up a boatload of bricks," I told Betty after making a short hike along the beach. The upper half of the tidal pile was uncovered. All we had to do was scrape off the barnacles and stow them in the dugout. They would be good ballast for *Skylark*. "We'll need them at Puffin Cove."

Betty found one good bottle—a real prize—about 3 inches tall, ¾ inch in diameter, and embossed with Chinese characters.

The morning sun sparkled on Lagoon Inlet's glassy surface. Patches of green showed on the burned-over hillsides.

In a small bight of Dana Passage we found a float camp moored to the trees. A rivulet supplied fresh water to the double-deck combination cookhouse and bunkhouse built on a large wooden barge. Adjacent, and connected by caulk-chewed walkways, were modest float homes for married loggers. One of the wives waved a cup, the international invitation for tea or coffee. We quickly tied up within two steps of the open kitchen door. Her son, playing on the float, wore a lifejacket. "It's part of his clothing," she said as we introduced ourselves. "He puts it on in the morning and takes it off at bedtime."

The house was neat and pleasant. With running water, an oil stove, and an electric generator, it had all the amenities of town plus the beauty of a wilderness waterfront home.

"I've always liked float houses," Betty said. "They have a freedom you don't find ashore."

"And no property taxes," I added.

Every two or three years the camp was towed to a new location, providing new scenery without the inconvenience of moving furniture or redecorating.

Our hostess tossed an empty condensed milk can out the window and into the salt chuck. Turning, she said, "We rented a place in town last winter, and for the first couple of days all my garbage went out the window. Then I had to clean up the yard." With a wry smile, she added, "I guess I'm just bushed, but I love this life."

Early that afternoon we anchored beside the sandy beach at Tanu. A mossy trail trodden only by deer, bear, and the occasional visitor led from the village through open forest to a small beach at the north. Midway there was a trench about twenty-five feet long and six feet wide, covered with poles and branches, overgrown with moss, and broken open by age. Inside were many bodies, probably smallpox victims, buried some eighty years before. Nearby was a lone marble marker inscribed: To Charlie.

This was the beautiful and well-situated village abandoned when the Haidas moved to New Clew, where Mathers Creek assured them of a year-round flow of pure water, a ready supply of salmon and trout, and proximity to the village of Cumshewa.

Was there nothing but death and destruction in these unique islands? Today life and beauty abound. But for a century—ending about fifty years ago—epidemics had come close to annihilating the Haidas. Then missionary doctors brought smallpox, tuberculosis, and other white man's diseases under control, and the Haidas increased.

Hecate Strait was flat. "Let's go to the hotsprings," Gene said. We were tempted, but we wanted to explore the passages and waterways along this part of Moresby Island. We turned west into Richardson Passage, past miles of vigorous second-growth forest.

The ruins of Lockeport were beside us when we anchored for the night. Broken red bricks sprinkled the pebbled shore. A clearing and demolished foundations were evidence of a settlement that once included a mining recording office, a store, a post office, a cannery, and houses—business enough to attract a monthly freight and passenger ship.

We found bricks, broken glass, and bottles—always bottles. During an hour's search we discovered a few unbroken molded or embossed bottles.

The next morning a passing squall dumped buckets of

chill rain on us as we headed into Darwin Sound. Shuttle Island was dead ahead.

Over the years a number of claims had been staked here and some gold taken. In 1955 we happened by on the day three partners were closing down after investing about three thousand dollars and nearly three months of hard labor into the search for gold. Using a drag bucket to bring gravel up from the salt chuck, they ran it through a steel separator and then washed the sand and gravel down a series of riffles. Anything trapped in the riffles was swirled in a prospector's pan.

"Gene, do you remember when the prospectors gave you and George some gold?" Betty asked. The discouraged men had presented our bug-eyed boys with their final day's take of black sand and "color"—about a nickel's worth. Appropriately, it was contained in an aspirin bottle.

"Sure do. And I still have it."

By the time we entered Juan Perez Sound the unpredictable weather had, predictably, changed. The squally southeaster was veering to the west, becoming a dry breeze, ruffling the water and sweeping away the clouds. The dogs stretched out on deck and napped in the sun.

We took a narrow passage that zigzagged through the Bischof Islands, a low, verdant group of islands nestled around a pocket-sized anchorage where Haida families once camped in summer, fishing, digging clams, or prying abalone and purple-hinged rock scallops off rocks at low tide. Pigeon guillemots, common murres, and glaucous-winged gulls flew from our path. Black oyster catchers took to the air, screaming and fussing.

The day was warm enough to prevent steam from rising from the many hotsprings on the west side of Hotspring Island. There were no boats in sight, and no smoke was curling from the lone shake cabin. "The tub's all ours," Betty said, "for as long as we want it."

A wooden trough and thick rubber hose led to the cast-iron tub from two bubbling pools—one too hot; the other, just a little too cool. So we cleaned out the tub, mixed water from the two pools, and enjoyed a long, relaxing soak.

While I parboiled, Betty carved our names and the date into a wide cedar shake. Similar carved shakes were nailed to the airy bathhouse—the guest registry, the boaters' seal of approval, to be read while one was submerged to the chin in sulfurous water.

"Glad we got this engine," I said after boarding *Skylark*. "So far it's used about ten gallons. At that rate we could cruise around the Charlottes at least once before refueling."

Lazy rollers washed under the port bow as we crossed the southern side of Juan Perez Sound. Without warning, a whale shot straight into the air about a quarter-mile away. It hung between sea and sky for an instant and then crashed onto its side with a resounding splash.

"Whale!" I bellowed. Betty and Gene were on deck in time to see the spectacular performance twice repeated. Then it expelled a spout of moist vapor about fifteen feet high, waved its broad flukes, and sounded.

"That was a humpback whale," said Betty, the family whale specialist.

To me, the sight of a leaping whale is a greater thrill than seeing the hometown team win its first-ever victory.

The chart showed a small seamount north of All Alone Stone, a likely spot to catch our supper. Gene tossed his jig over the port side; I tried the starboard. Gulls voiced encouragement as cloud shadows drifted by.

"Got one!" Gene yelled, hauling in fathoms of two-hundred-pound-test monofilament and heaving a flopping thirty-inch lingcod on deck. The dogs barked and danced.

"That's all we need," Betty said, already planning how she would cook it.

"Let's make up our lines and get underway," I said. "I'd like to catch one too, but they'll keep better in the sea and there's no need to waste them."

Skylark ceased rolling as we entered Burnaby Strait. Moresby Island lay to starboard; Huxley, then Burnaby Island, to port. A long, curving scar marked Huxley where logging had cleared a steep sidehill.

A check of the tide tables and chart showed we could slip through the Dolomite Narrows. Three vertical white boards were the improvised navigation aids.

Gene went forward, the eighteen-foot aluminum pike pole—marked for taking soundings—in hand. I slowed to half speed. The bottom shoaled fast. Gene indicated the channel, and I spun the helm to port. Pointing to rocks on both bows, Gene called, "Rocks below! I think we'll miss them."

I hoped so. Another hard turn to starboard, and we were safely through the shallowest part.

"Look!" Gene pointed ahead to an islet where three dwarf trees grew. A bear lurched into the water and swam toward a larger island, his thick-furred back well out of the water, his head high. Sitka started barking, and Ivan howled. The bear stopped on the rocks and gave a mighty shake before jogging into the forest.

"He'd be a real trophy, Gene. But I hope he gets to die of old age."

Bag Harbour, a small bay surrounded by cedars with a salmon stream fanning across flat rocks at the far end, was our anchorage for the night. A rusted boiler, remains of a pre-World War II Japanese clam cannery, lay on the beach. Broken, bleached clamshells were piled on the gravel. Alders now covered the old clearing. As we approached, a deer skittered into the woods and sea ducks paddled away.

"That's where George got his first buck," Gene said, pointing to the north shore.

"It's not every twelve-year-old that gets to be the family hunter—and succeeds at it." George was the hunter and fisherman on our 1955 trip. Gene was scientist and artist.

Another clear, bright sunrise. "How much more of this California weather are we going to have?" I asked as Gene hauled in the anchor. "This is as good as anything we had during our first trip."

"Let's take advantage of every minute," Betty said.

Skylark seemed to glide across Skincuttle Inlet as we headed toward Jedway. An ivory plume of alder smoke spiraled from our "Charlie Noble." Gulls argued as they fed in kelp patches, where tapiocalike herring spawn covered the submerged leaves.

Japanese characters on bow and counter gave name and home port of the large ore carrier loading at the floating dock. A brown haze drifted from her raked stack. Stocky sailors, heads wrapped with sweat towels and clothes splattered with paint, worked from stages rigged over the high, straight sides, chipping, wire brushing, and touching up the ship with black paint. A thick hose of iron concentrate fell from the goose-necked loader into the ship's cavernous bowels. Her Plimsoll mark was a fathom above the sea.

We rowed ashore to see friends and purchase fresh-baked bread, plus a few other items we had overlooked.

"The mine's closing down" were the first words we heard. "Closing this fall. No later than spring."

That seemed a normal pattern in the Charlottes: build today; leave tomorrow. Nearly all the evidence of humans we had seen on this trip was in the form of abandoned ruins. The Haidas had left because of disease and death; the Europeans, for economic reasons.

Shortly after noon we were underway, passing first the ore ship and then an acre of so of waste rock spilling into the inlet. Hecate Strait welcomed us with a silvery, rippled surface.

At Benjamin Point we searched for some glass balls that Betty and Gene had cached—but to no avail. Someone must have come ashore and found them.

Entering Rose Harbour, we anchored in front of an

abandoned whaling station, where patches of tall daffodils brightened an extensive clearing. We began searching for bottles along the gravel beach and around the rotting foundations of tumbled bunkhouses. Before dusk, we were hitting pay dirt.

"This is even better than I hoped for," Betty said, uncovering a crockery container with an opening at the top and a pouring spout. "I'd like to stay another day or two."

"Let's let the weather decide. If it's calm, we go; stormy, we stay."

Betty must have been saying her prayers. Toward morning the splatter of raindrops on the cabin roof awakened me. From the station came the clatter of torn galvanized roofing flopping in the rising wind.

Betty was happy to dig in the rain, putting to use the archaeological training she had received at the University of British Columbia while I was off the coast of Korea with Task Force 77. As our collection increased, Gene and I began to enjoy digging. We decided to stay for a third day, even though the weather calmed.

The majority of the bottles and crocks we found were broken. Some had broken when they were discarded; others, when entrapped water froze. There were colored bottles, clear bottles, big ones, small ones, embossed, plain, molded, blown, Chinese, Japanese, Canadian, American, and English bottles—all tossed out of the shoreworkers' bunkhouse. A few of the thin crockery containers survived intact. Pieces of buttons and worked sperm teeth lay hidden in the dump.

"Okay, you've got enough crocks and bottles," I said, "and I'll bet you don't have a clue what you'll do with any of them!"

"Yes I do!" But Betty didn't tell us.

We went on to Puffin Cove, unloaded the bricks, and enjoyed a few days there before catching a week of calm seas on our way to Sandspit. We were refreshed and ready for more work on the house addition.

4

Gyppo Logging

We had just seen the first geese winging their way south. Fall gales would soon take the pleasure out of cruising, and there was no chance of starting construction at Puffin Cove until next spring. We had spent too much time beachcombing and photographing, as well as taking two groups of scientists, from the University of British Columbia and the University of Uppsala in Sweden, on charters to study mosses and bogs.

We were enjoying the extra space of the house addition. Gene had a small sleeping loft in a window-lit corner behind the fireplace; it was warm, cozy, and private. His books lined the shelves on one wall, and a lamp usually burned until after midnight.

One day Leo Saarnok stopped by. Leo is a heavily muscled man of about six-two with shoulders any fullback would envy. His eyes are dark and alert beneath his bushy brows. The corners of his generous mouth curve upward, and he smiles easily. Although he was in his midfifties at the time, he was a formidable worker and surefooted on a floating log.

"Want to go logging with me?" he asked over the inevitable cup of coffee. We were sitting in front of the big fireplace, where blazing spruce logs warmed the nearly completed living room.

Gene was in top physical condition and ready to go. I was neither eager nor in shape.

Leo and his wife, Evie, were Estonians. During World War II they had escaped from Estonia on foot, taking only what they could carry, and had crossed the Baltic Sea to Sweden on an overloaded fishing boat. They emigrated to eastern Canada, where Leo worked as a lumberjack. Then they moved on to the Queen Charlottes, where Leo became a faller. But his heart was always on a logging company of his own.

Betty first met the Saarnoks at their camp in Skidegate Narrows when she was on a dugout canoe trip. After Gene and I arrived, we spent a day taking movies and slides of Leo's operation. Many of the trees contained enough wood to build a frame house. All were hauled out with a Cat and an arch—a lot different from my days in the Michigan woods, where we felled and bucked with a seven-foot crosscut saw and dragged our small logs with a team of horses. Only the danger remained the same. Or had that increased?

Because of the danger, I was reluctant to see Gene go logging. I had faith in Leo, but how about some of his help? The hard work would be good for me; the pay, good for the bank account.

Small companies like Leo's do contract work for the large companies, logging areas that are too far from the main camp to be economical for truck logging. Small operators set up camp, log for a year or two, and then move to the next claim—if they are efficient enough to make money and don't run into a streak of bad luck. Often called gyppos, these companies vary widely in living conditions, hours of work, quality of food, and rate of pay. Sometimes the pay never materializes; the companies just go broke.

"The expenses come every day," Leo told me, "but days to earn—not so many."

Leo let me refill his cup. "Take your choice: union wages, or go contract at three dollars a thousand—each. Some days we should put fifty thousand board feet of timber in the salt chuck. Other days we'll be broken down."

I glanced at Gene. He nodded. "We'll go contract." It was an incentive to finish quickly, to be home by Christmas.

"Evie and I have moved the camp. Need you to give us a hand setting up. Then we'll be ready when fisheries says okay," Leo said at the door.

Early in October we made the hour-long trip to Long Inlet—Long Arm to most residents—aboard *Islander*, Leo's forty-foot steel-hulled tug.

Three log floats were moored to the trees. Each float was made of spruce logs about four feet through the butt and sixty feet long, laid end to top and laced tightly with wire rope. The floats were about thirty feet wide. One held the cookhouse and a workshop; another, an old bunkhouse; and a third, two Cats and a rubber-tired arch.

On a level place near the river mouth, Leo bulldozed hummocks of salt grass and gravel, making a flat place in the slough for the two camp floats and *Skylark*.

During the hour of October's highest tide, we shoved the two house floats into their snug haven, mooring each float to large stumps with wire and tying them side by side. For only two to six hours a day during the spring tides—the exceptionally high tides that come about twice a month at the time of the new moon and the full moon—would they be afloat.

The cookhouse, with a small bedroom for Leo and Evie, was the largest and newest structure. Gene and I had the old bunkhouse. The workshop was a ramshackle shed whose door had flown off in one of the island's wilder storms.

It was mid-October before a fisheries officer inspected the

inlet and decided that no more salmon were waiting to enter the stream.

"You can start logging anytime." We had been waiting for those words.

We spent the first day in camp rigging the bag to hold our floating logs. This entailed stringing about twenty-four boom-sticks—each sixty-six feet long and connected end to end by iron boom chains—in a loose half-circle free to rise and fall with the tide.

"Do this right," Leo said, "and we won't lose any logs. Do it wrong, and our money drifts out the inlet." One end was anchored near an undercut gravel bank; the other, tied to an angled outcrop of jagged rock. The river current would always carry the logs away from the bank, preventing them from piling on top of each other when we rolled them in.

Leo's two Cats were both D-7s. "The old Cat's insurance," he explained, "in case the new one gets stalled in a mud hole or mired on the tide flats and can't winch itself out." As it turned out, we only needed the old Cat once, and it paid for itself in less than an hour. The new Cat went over the river bank and couldn't crawl out without assistance.

Evie, a handsome chestnut-haired woman with fine features and smiling eyes, was the cook. Her life in a logging camp was far different from her well-heeled life in Estonia, but she had adapted quickly. It was amazing to watch her walk the unsteady floating boomsticks—especially in high heels. She would hold on to Leo's wide leather belt and place her tiny feet right behind his, never looking right or left, as they boarded or left *Islander*.

One day I commented on this, and Leo said: "Yes, eyes closed, that's the way she followed me through a battlefield littered with dead Germans and Russians when we escaped."

Cat logging was new to Gene and me, so the first couple of days we struggled along without moving many logs from hillside to salt water. Leo patiently showed us how to work the knob of a wire choker under a log and connect it to the bell, forming a sliding loop; how to set a rolling hitch so a log would roll over a stump or rock; how to rig the choker so the log would first move endwise before turning; how to plan our work and get all adjacent logs in one turn, or load; how to get two logs with one choker; and how to estimate what the Cat could pull under various conditions. We learned that by watching the crawler tracks revolve without moving forward; it wasn't a scheduled lesson.

We worked on the lower slopes of a two-thousand-foot mountain. Inland the peaks exceeded three thousand feet. The low, weak autumnal sun never rose above those bare ridges to shine on us; we were always in the shade. Across the stream we could see the lukewarm afternoon sun shining on a village site where Haidas once lived.

We were also in the mountain's rain shadow. Although the Charlottes have a reputation for excessive rain, in our camp it was wetter than its reputation. In one way the rain was an advantage: all of our fresh water was collected in tubs from the cookhouse eaves. Although a stream passed within yards of the float, it stunk of spawned-out salmon. "Like rotten fish soup" was Leo's apt description.

The fall days were short. Evie would rouse us by calling from the cookhouse window. Dressing in the dark, we would cross the damp, sometimes frosty, always slippery logs to the cookhouse for coffee, followed by a hearty breakfast to order—enough to keep us working most of the day. Somewhere along the way Evie found time to load our lunchboxes.

Dawn arrived about the time we finished lacing up our caulked boots and were struggling into our rain gear. Fair weather or foul, we would get wet soon enough just lying on the ground thrusting those reluctant choker knobs under a big log.

Leo drove the Cat. I sat on a tool box beside him, and Gene rode on top of the fuel tank, holding on to bars supporting the steel safety roof. The trail—it couldn't be called a road—snaked and churned across a series of rivulets, their size depending on the previous hour's weather, and then through a mud hole where the Cat sunk to its engine bed, across chewed roots and between stumps scarred by frequent jousts with the Cat's blade. We jolted across small logs, treetops, and limbs. It was a slow, jarring journey, but it was infinitely better than slogging afoot across that desolate no-man's-land.

While Leo turned the Cat and big arch around, Gene and I hauled out the wire chokers and looped them around the nearest logs. Leaving Gene to do the last few, I would haul out the main line that ran from the Cat's winch through a fairlead at the top of the high arch. Leo watched, a cigar poking from his mouth, as he moved operating levers that looked like toys in his ham-sized hands. He never wore caulked boots while driving the Cat, just gum boots. "Feels the foot pedals better," he said.

After individually winching anywhere from one to a dozen logs—depending on their size—into a pile behind the arch, we would loop the eye of the chokers onto a big G-shaped hook. Leo then winched in until the front ends of the logs were lifted well off the ground. The arch half carried, half dragged the logs, moving more than twice as much timber as would be possible by dragging, and eliminating the chance that a log would become hung up on a rock or stump and split, or that expensive chokers would snap.

As Leo roared away, Gene and I set the second batch of chokers, starting with the easy logs. Logs lying on uneven ground were no problem. Others lay in a few inches of mud, where roots or limbs hindered our attempts to punch a hole for the choker knob. Some of these logs took one of us on each side.

Sometimes we would have to loop the wire over an end, knowing it would slip off, in the hopes that the log would move enough so that we could choke it properly. A few times we would ask Leo to use the hydraulic blade to lift or shove a log. Some logs—usually Sitka spruce—were so large we had to stand on tiptoe to see across—and I'm a fraction of an inch under six feet.

If the logs were straight grained and knot free, they could be sold as premium peeler logs, used for plywood manufacturing. A few of these lovely brutes required two chokers hooked together to fit around them. We all liked those beauties of five thousand to eight thousand board feet. "I can see big neon dollar signs flashing on them," I told Gene.

Once the chokers were set, we were free to dive into our lunchboxes and see what goodies Evie had prepared to go with our steaming tea or coffee. This was often the signal for a pair of ravens to fly in, entertain us with a few complicated acrobatics, and remind us that they too liked Evie's cooking.

Ravens and rain were the reasons we used metal boxes. One logger friend used a paper bag until the ravens found it hidden under a log and flew away with a few sandwiches and, worse, his new set of dentures. "Had to go back to getting my nourishment out of a bottle," he told us with a toothless smile.

Leo always returned with a smile. Pulling the cheroot out of his face, he would often tell a joke—the type you could repeat anywhere. Or he would start off with, "Old Swede says...." Leo always said something to make us laugh and to make work more pleasant. Only once did we catch him repeating himself.

Somewhere around midday—between turns— we would settle back against a stump and enjoy lunch. The ravens might miss the morning or afternoon coffee break, but they never missed lunch. They would zoom in squawking and settle nearby to wait for a crust or whatever. After we moved away they would glide in and grab what was left.

Sometime during the day, depending on the tides, we would ride down with Leo to saw or chop off any remaining limbs and stamp both ends of all logs lying on the bank with Leo's brand. Instead of a cattleman's burning iron, we used a light sledge with a combination of numbers and letters embossed on its head. Both ends of every log had to be hit at least twice so that however it floated, Leo's brand would be visible to scaler and buyer. When all the logs were stamped, Leo shoved them into the water, where they were trapped within the boomsticks.

At dusk, about five o'clock, we would hook on the last turn for the day and ride to camp. Every other evening we stopped by the fuel dump, where Gene and I pumped diesel fuel from forty-five-gallon drums into the Cat's tank while Leo worked over lube fittings.

Usually Gene and I waded into the stream by camp to wash the thick mud from our boots, pants, and rain gear. That bone-chilling stream was more than refreshing. Then it was a fast trot to our oil-heated bunkhouse to strip, hang our leather boots and dripping clothes on a rack above the stove, and get into clean, dry clothes.

By the time we were presentable, Evie would call us to supper. *Banquet* is a more accurate word. There was all we could eat and more. Evie's thick sauerkraut soup, slowly cooked for hours in a great covered kettle and slathered with sour cream, is something I still dream about. Seldom could I slow down before consuming three bowls full. Then Evie served the meal!

After fighting my way from the table, I would return to the bunkhouse to read, grease my caulked boots, or rest. Gene usually waited for Leo to add his tally record. He kept count of the number of logs put in the water each day along with an estimate of their volume.

After flicking his cigar at an improvised ashtray labeled "Kippered Snacks," Leo would reach for the chessboard. For hours he and Gene would sit under the hanging Coleman gas lantern, one on each side of the four-foot-by-eight-foot plywood table, hunched forward, intently studying the chessmen before making each deliberate move. They were totally oblivious to the hissing lantern or to Evie, who would be working around the stove and sink. If Gene wasn't playing chess, he was studying one of his many chess books, planning how to beat the boss next time.

One evening, after a mug of coffee and warm chocolate cake, I scared something on the float. A galvanized tub rattled against a chain saw. "Leo, shoot the flashlight out here," I said, peering into the gloom of a chill, starlit night. "I think our coon is back." The previous night a raccoon had raided the food cache and eaten or broken two cartons of eggs.

The light swung across the float. "Don't think I'll go hunting with you," Leo boomed. "You don't know a little coon from a big bear!"

On the edge of the float, about fifteen feet away, a full-grown black bear, his fur thick and glossy, stood looking over his shoulder at us. A moment later he gracefully leaped to the beach and, with long, easy strides, disappeared beyond flashlight range.

"I don't like bears on the float," Evie said.

"Just yell. Say 'boo,' " Leo advised her. "They'll leave. Never heard of one attacking anybody in these islands."

We had seen bear tracks around the camp since the first light snowfall. Two days earlier, while we were in the bush, Evie had chased a yearling cub away from our open-air meat cooler. That week a bear chomped on the corner of a red plastic gas container I had stowed alongside a big stump. I had to hike back to camp for more fuel before we could finish bucking (cutting a felled tree into saw log lengths) and limbing a few wind-toppled trees.

We worked every day, weather permitting; it took a real gale to keep us in camp. Nevertheless, there were times of breakdown or interruptions—forest rangers flying in to inspect or a buyer dickering for Leo's timber claims and equipment. At these times Gene and I bucked and limbed or hiked through the wide valley filled with giant spruce and cedars and drained by the knee-deep salmon stream. Mallards jetted and quacked into the air when we surprised them at a bend. Sometimes we would see a bear feeding on the carcass of a spawned-out salmon.

One day while we were riding down to stamp some big logs, water and mud began to gurgle and suck around the drive hubs of the Cat. Abruptly the Cat lurched and swerved to the left before Leo could stop it.

"What's wrong, Leo?" I asked, reluctantly stepping into the deep mud.

"Track's off." Leo yanked free a broken spruce root that had snagged the track and thrown it off the drive sprocket. "We can fix it."

By late afternoon we knew how to remount crawler tracks half-submerged under cold, muddy water. That's a lesson you won't pick up in any classroom.

It was a lesson we were to appreciate two weeks later when, on a rocky hillside, the Cat slipped, caught on a sharp rock and cast the opposite track, coming to rest with the front end up at an angle of about twenty degrees and leaning fifteen degrees. When we arrived, Leo was kneeling on the thin snow peering at the track and sprocket. An unlit cigar rolled from side to side in his generous mouth.

"What now, Leo?" I asked, wishing we could winch the seventeen-ton machine into a level position.

Leo didn't rant and rave, curse, or madly throw tools around. He quietly put a massive box wrench on the adjusting nut and, bracing, pulled till his face was the color of the setting summer sun.

Nothing moved. "She's rusted tight. I'll have to burn it off—and I'm out of acetylene." He stretched his back. "Old Swede says, 'If you can't do one job, then do something else.' "

That's when I first suspected Leo was the originator of all those Old Swede aphorisms.

Leo looked at his watch and then at the sullen sky, where low clouds scudded northwest. "I'll have to go to town for another bottle of acetylene. Evie was saying she wants more fresh groceries. You can come along or stay."

"I want to go bear hunting," said Gene.

"Okay. We'll stay here."

When they returned two days later, Leo brought with him another hydraulic jack. A day of hard, often frustrating work, and we were again logging. The snow was gone, no longer hiding rocky outcroppings.

Before dusk one evening a pair of whistling swans with their three cygnets swept in for a sliding landing and spent a few days feeding and resting within sight of the cookhouse. Twice we saw them wade into the stream—all in a line— a snow-white adult at front and rear, the light gray-brown young carefully supervised. All held their long necks straight as they floated regally downstream, rising and dipping in the riffles as one might do on a merry-go-round.

A few frosty mornings later, as I crossed to the cook-house, I noticed the swans were gone. And so were our logs— every one!

With his binoculars, Leo spotted a broken boomstick. Beyond, our logs drifted about the inlet on the flooding tide. We rushed silently through breakfast. We had little appetite but knew we would need plenty of energy.

At the log dump we looked at the broken boomstick, one end on the rock, where it settled as the tide gently fell from under.

"Damned teredoes!" I exclaimed. Those destructive marine borers had left only the outer shell of the boomstick. Twisting and turning as they fed, they had filled the inner wood with pencil-sized holes. Viewed end on, the broken area of the stick looked like a sieve.

"I'll go to South Bay for new boomsticks," Leo said quietly, as though seeing ten to twelve thousand dollars' worth of logs drifting away was an everyday thing. Only the cheroot rolling from side to side in his mouth betrayed his agitation. "You two use the skiff and round up as many logs as your can."

Fortunately, two bags of logs had already been delivered and sold. Gene and I were paid according to the log scaler's tally. A few days more, and we would have had another two hundred thousand board feet in that bag.

Evie was in town getting ready for Christmas. This was hardly a present for her. Betty was cooking in camp. She slid her dugout into the salt chuck to help. It was desperately hard, slow work, but she managed to shove or tow five good logs into the repaired bag.

Most of that mizzly day Gene and I towed logs with the little outboard. At best, logs are obstinate things. We recovered the larger ones first. Some drifted ashore, pushed by the afternoon wind; others, we shoved. Most continued inexorably out the inlet. The tide was now flooding, but the wind took our logs out.

Late in the afternoon we heard the welcome sound of *Islander's* diesel. "Got forty sticks," Leo yelled, waving at the long, sinuous line of logs following him as we came alongside. "We'll block off the inlet."

We rigged the boomsticks across the inlet's throat, both ends tied to sturdy trees. Now our logs were all corralled within Long Inlet. It was dark and we had not eaten since breakfast. Tired and dispirited, we returned to camp.

Dawn and high tide arrived together. We walked the beaches, pushing the floating logs away from shore with long pike poles. The ebbing tide carried them down the windless inlet toward our barrier of boomsticks. Nature was working for us. At low slack we would join both ends of the boomsticks and tow our catch back to camp. We would be out only a couple days of work. A light wind rose, speeding the logs toward the inlet's choked-off entrance. Our luck was improving. For the first time in two days Leo joked. Gene and I laughed.

We were at the booming grounds, shoving logs retrieved the previous day into a small pocket, making room for all those we would soon tow back.

"How did *that* get over there?" I pointed at a scruffy gill net boat moving slowly along the opposite shore. It was a stupid question. The answer was too obvious.

Leo took a fast look and slammed *Islander* into reverse. Gene leaped from a boomstick, caught the gunwale of the moving tug, and hauled himself aboard. I threw a couple turns of the skiff's painter around the towing bitts.

Islander roared toward the entrance, dodging drifting logs. Gulls, murres, guillemots, and ducks fled. We had never considered the possibility that someone would pull the toggle link connecting our boomsticks, allowing them to swing open like hinged gates. Only two boats had come into the inlet during the past six weeks; it was not as if we were blocking some busy marine way.

There was no hope of reconnecting the boomsticks against the ebbing tide. Using tug and skiff, we rounded up the largest logs, driving a dog—a type of staple—with a line spliced to it into the end of each log before tying it onto a long towline. Progress was slow.

About three hours later Leo noticed the gill netter chugging down the far side. "Throw off the towline," he ordered. We charged toward the troublemakers. *Islander's* screw churned the water into froth as we rocked to a stop in their path. The two Indians stopped and stared sullenly at us. Hunting rifles lay across the hatch within easy reach, although no deer or other game was in sight.

I had never heard Leo swear, but with over ten thousand dollars' worth of logs adrift I was expecting some harsh words.

"Why?" Leo spoke quietly.

The Indians were as surprised as I. They muttered something about deer hunting and prospecting and said that we had no right to block off the inlet.

We were wasting time, and there was none to be wasted.

Too many dollars were drifting out the inlet. If we were to retrieve more logs, we would have to do it within the next two hours, before dark.

"I could have bought you a steer," Leo said, calling the two men by name, "or paid for all your meals at Marg's Café till next spring—and still been money ahead if you hadn't opened my boom."

While the Indians stared dumbfounded, *Islander's* diesel screamed, white water frothing around her stern. We leaned into a tight turn.

The gaslight was bright in the cookhouse when we came up the frosty, starlit inlet with our pitiful tow. Even the steaming beef stew Betty generously ladled onto our platters did little to dispel our gloom.

Leo's jokes were infrequent the next few days. That had been a senseless loss for all of us.

Another ten days, and all felled timber was in the water. Christmas was a couple of weeks away. We tried to cut our losses by dropping a few more big trees and bucking up all blowdowns from an early October gale. This meant staying in camp longer than we had planned. We thrived on Betty's camp cookery and some off-the-cuff dishes concocted from assorted leftovers.

This was also the year when cones were being purchased for reseeding logged or burned-off lands in the States. A bag of spruce cones went for five dollars; a bag of the much smaller hemlock cones, for twenty dollars. Betty picked cones from the newly felled trees. It was slow, prickly work, often done in chilling rain.

Falling, bucking, limbing, and hauling out the logs lent diversity to each day's work. One blowdown spruce about three feet through the butt lay on the flats, its shallow root structure standing on edge like a great, black ten-foot-high plate. As my chain saw snarled through the last of the butt cut, the roots and stump swung back and flopped into place as if mounted on spring-loaded hinges. I had to look closely to see where some small outer roots had slipped from under the surrounding moss. What if I had left my lunch bucket or gas can there? A logger could have been killed.

A few days before Christmas the Cats and arch were parked by the fuel dump for the last time. Betty and Gene headed for Sandspit in *Skylark*, while Leo and I boarded *Islander* to tow our last bag of logs to South Bay.

Towing is drearily slow even when you are moving with the tide. Low clouds and heavy rain did not help. When we reached Renner Pass, at dusk, the tide was turning against us.

"We'll tie up for the night," Leo said. I was more than agreeable. Leo shoved the logs against the shore. With a coil of line over my shoulder, I scrambled across the logs and secured our tow to a tree. After a quick meal from tin cans, we tumbled into our bunks.

We rose at four the next morning, the first day of winter. Leo shoved a giant-sized jar of Polski dill pickles into my face, saying, "Have some." I can eat nearly anything, anytime, but never a pickle as an eye-opener.

I cast off the shoreline, and we hauled away from the beach. The tide was with us. A few hours later we tied up the logs and boomsticks at South Bay and turned toward home— at full speed.

Leo's career in logging was over. After only a few years of hard work, he and Evie had succeeded in Canada. They were ready to move to Vancouver and invest in high-rise apartment buildings.

We laughed and joked as *Islander* charged up Skidegate Inlet. The air was nippy, and snow brightened the trees on the higher slopes. The sky was darkening. "Looks like we'll have snow in Sandspit for Christmas," I said. And, when the logs were scaled and sold, another healthy check.

Sunny California, crowded freeways, and regular working hours were a long way off.

5

Big Black Bear

Soon after we began logging with Leo in Long Inlet, Gene told me he wanted to go bear hunting. Neither of us had ever shot a bear, and I wasn't sure I wanted to. I was hoping to bag a few ducks. We had our chance when Leo and Evie went into Queen Charlotte City for acetylene and groceries.

During October and November large flocks of mallards, scaups, goldeneyes, and scoters arrived, feeding and fattening along the shoreline and up the salmon stream. Canada geese sometimes circled, honking loudly. They never landed near camp.

After leaving the logging camp, Gene and I picked up a game trail along the mossy edge of the winding stream. Ducks quacked continually, and at times we caught a glimpse of one or more winging above the tall spruce trees. Low salal and the occasional clump of viciously prickly devil's club thrived in this virgin forest.

Suddenly a brace of loud mallards flew over the stream. The flashy drake in front presented a straight-away shot. I fired, and he tumbled. Another duck, a female, was turning downstream. My automatic roared, and the duck fell onto the far shore.

"Hold this and watch that duck." I thrust the empty shotgun at Gene. Running along the trail until I was ahead of the fast-drifting drake, I slid down the steep gravel bank and into the chill water. Then I looked for the duck. Her modest colors blended with the rocks.

Gene realized my problem. "Ahead, and to your right."

I hefted both ducks proudly. "A nice fat pair!"

"Yes, and you just got yourself a job." Gene stretched the drake's wings, admiring their multicolored beauty. "You'll have to clean them. I don't know how." He didn't sound eager to learn.

After tying a cord around the feet of both birds, I hung them over a spruce branch to bleed. "We'll pick them up on the way back."

Each fall thousands of chum salmon return to this stream to spawn. Now only a few dozen late arrivals lay in the pools, slowly working their way upstream, their three-to-five-year life cycle nearly complete. The bodies of spawned-out salmon drifted in the back eddies. Some were caught in a tangle of branches and leaves from toppled trees lying across the stream.

Salmon, dead or alive, bring normally unsociable bears to congregate along every salmon stream. Bones, skin, and gill covers lay on the mossy banks.

The quacking of an approaching mallard alerted us. I stepped into an open area. The mallard was alone, difficult to spot as it flew low over the shadow-dappled water. For a moment it was caught in a shaft of light—a mallard drake. Spotting me just as I squeezed the trigger, he quickly changed course. He was climbing steeply when the second shot struck him. With wings outstretched, he volplaned onto the opposite shore.

"Three's plenty for supper," I said, hanging him from a trailside tree.

The bright afternoon sky had clouded over, and what had appeared to be a passing shower was now a steady drizzle. Only in the Charlottes can weather change so abruptly. At first the trees afforded protection. Now large, accumulated drops splattered us.

"We'll be soaked before we reach camp," I said, watching smoke-gray clouds scud above the treetops. "So we might as well keep after your bear. Rain may even help us."

I reloaded the shotgun with rifled slugs. Gene watched me quizzically.

"It's not much of a big-game weapon, but it'll do for backup."

In this valley "small timber" meant trees less than three feet through the butt. Many of the soaring spruce were five to seven feet across, and a few exceeded ten feet. As we walked, I imagined the Haidas stalking a big bruin, walking under the same ancient trees; spearing or netting salmon in a stream choked with fish; and always alert for a large, straight, high-limbed cedar to be carved into an oceangoing dugout canoe or a totem pole.

Soft, springy sphagnum moss covered the ground and fallen trees. Lacy lichens hung from limbs, reminding me of the laundry drying on bamboo poles I had seen in China. Along the twisting stream, scraggly alders, not much larger than bushes, provided browse for a doe and her twins. A black-crested Steller's jay scolded us, its low-pitched, raucous call repeated again and again.

Fresh bear sign was all about: tracks, manure, and pieces of chewed-on salmon. "Lots of bears around here, Gene. You won't have to take the first one we see."

"I doubt if another human's been here for years," Gene said when we were about three miles upstream.

"You must have missed that red tape on a small spruce a

ways back. Probably timber cruisers. Some gyppo will be logging this in a couple years. Leo has a claim to sell up here somewhere."

We crossed a midstream gravel bar, where a dozen alders held a tenuous existence. Suddenly Gene stopped, motioning me to do the same.

"What's up?" I whispered, forgetting that the tumbling stream and dripping trees would muffle anything less than a piercing scream.

Gene pointed to what might have been a large, dark rock about a hundred yards ahead, beyond an old windfall lying across the stream.

The object moved. Its head came up. A massive black bear! I was glad I had loaded the shotgun with rifled slugs. Slowly, deliberately, without a thought of danger, the bear went about his fishing. This fellow was not content with anything less than fresh salmon. He stood belly-deep in a pool, peering at frightened salmon, and then moved to a more advantageous position.

We stared, fascinated by this poacher, who waited with mouth slightly open, his long red tongue darting across his black lips. A lightning lunge, and his head was under water. In an instant, with speed belying his size, he jerked back, mouth closed—and empty. A loose necklace of pearly spray flew as he shook that gigantic head.

Were live, egg- or milt-filled salmon that much tastier than the dead ones drifting downstream? I knew my choice, but I didn't think any bear was so persnickety.

The bear now stood broadside to us. Gene planned his strategy. "Let's move up to that log. Could get him from here, but I want to be sure of a clean kill." Gene smoothly worked the bolt, chambered a round, and set the safety.

The bear turned his broad rump toward us. We moved. An old log, studded with jagged stubs of broken limbs, provided a mossy bench rest for the .30-'06. Gene aimed across open sights. His trophy was less than seventy-five feet away–and looking as big as the proverbial barn door. I wondered how many hunters had missed at this range.

That bear had looked big at first sighting. Now I said to myself, "Neil, that's the biggest black bear you've ever seen. Maybe the biggest you'll ever see."

I thought of our first trip to the Charlottes and of meeting Jack Fraser, an experienced outdoorsman and big-game guide. While displaying skulls from bears he had shot, Jack predicted that the world's record would someday be taken from these islands. Were we looking at a record breaker?

Gene was ready, waiting for a better angle. The bear moved slowly about the pool, intent on snapping his jaws into a live salmon. At last, after what seemed like a half-hour but was probably only two or three minutes, he turned to face us, head up, nose twitching.

The rifle boomed, shattering the valley's murmuring. The bear dropped. The reverberations died, and the valley was quiet.

"Good shooting! Where did you hit him?"

"The brain." Gene chambered another round and began to climb over the windfall.

"Wait. We'll stay here a couple minutes. Just to make sure he's dead. And you may have fouled up a record skull."

The time passed slowly. We saw no movement and approached from the rear, safeties off. I poked the inert form with a limb. "A good clean kill, Gene. Congratulations!"

The head and chest of this old boar were scarred, his broad shoulders nearly hairless. The tip of his left ear had been snipped off in some wild forest fight. The right ear, ripped from skull to tip, hung in limp, hairy strips. The broken lower right canine tooth dangled from a thin section of healed-over gum. All of the bear's teeth were discolored and badly worn.

"That must have been some toothache! Bet he was hard to get along with." Gene pulled out his knife and sliced off the jagged tooth.

"I suspect he was the big *honshu* in these parts, " I said, lifting the head to get a full view of it. "I've never seen such a big brute. This could be the world's record Jack talked about."

"I'm going to make this hide into a rug. It'll keep my feet warm when I get out of bed on cold mornings."

Dusk comes before 5:00 p.m. near the end of November in this north country. Steady rain and thick clouds were now hastening it. I was soaked and shivering. "It'll be pitch black before we can skin him out, so let's blaze this alder and come back in the morning—with the packboard and camera."

"Okay." Gene dropped the right front paw after pointing out a missing pad and claw. "I'm cold too. Let's go".

Gene was silent as we hurried along the darkening trail. At last he said, "I have my bear—maybe even a record skull— but I don't think I'll ever shoot another one." I turned, and our eyes met as he continued. "That's going to make a big dent in the valley's population."

"He was thin." I understood Gene's concern for wildlife, and I was happy he didn't want to see how many more he could kill. "With winter coming on he might have slowly starved. It's possible you did the old fellow a favor, in a way."

Rain pelted our faces. Water squished in our caulked boots. Dusk had turned to darkness by the time we picked up our cached mallards.

Camp was black and warm. It didn't take long to towel down and climb into dry wool clothes. Gene pumped and lit the Coleman lantern while I turned up the oil stove to heat the oven and boil a big pot of coffee. Then I plucked and drew the ducks. No time for frills such as sage dressing. We were too hungry. I wiped the trio inside and out with plenty of butter, sprinkled them liberally with garlic and salt, laid a thick slice of bacon lengthwise on each as they lay breast-up in the roasting pan, and slid them into the oven. Potatoes, carrots, and onions would go in later.

Rain hammered on the cookhouse roof and black window

panes. Wind rattled the window frames. An empty fuel drum overturned with a bang. A growing puddle sneaked under the door.

"How much longer?" Gene looked up from his chess book. "I could eat two of those myself!"

We were both even hungrier by the time the sound of sputtering fat came from the oven, joining the tantalizing aroma of roast duck.

At last! The sizzling pan was on the table between us. This was Gene's first taste of wild duck. "Don't crack your teeth on the shot," I warned, placing a steaming, fat drake on his platter. Only wing tips and bony necks survived our famished onslaught.

The pounding of gale-driven rain on the thick shake roof awakened me sometime during the night. I enjoyed the sound. I was dry, warm, and well-fed. I thought of the television programs in which we had once found vicarious adventure and of California's shopping centers, where nearly anything could be purchased. I fell asleep, contented.

Sometime before dawn the rain ceased. The wind veered, becoming a fresh westerly, sweeping away dark clouds, and leaving a clean, bright blue sky. I recalled Leo's saying: "The west wind is the sky's broom."

We set off for the stream. My camera was in the packboard; Gene cradled the rifle. Honed knives hung on our hips. Well over two inches of rain had fallen during the past sixteen hours, and our quiet stream was a wild, foaming river, overflowing its banks and flooding the lowlands. Limbs, small alders, and other woodland debris mixed with hundreds of spawned-out salmon, all hurtling seaward in the muddy current.

"This doesn't look good for skinning out—or even finding—your bear," I reluctantly conceded. Gene didn't answer. He didn't have to. We both knew who had suggested leaving it overnight.

Skirting the flooded lowlands, we reached the fallen spruce Gene had used as a bench rest. It was nearly covered with agitated water. "There's the blazed tree," said Gene, pointing. Without that we might have missed the pool. There was no sign of any bear. We jabbed broken limbs into the eddying water—and touched only gravel.

"I'll search downstream, on the other side," Gene said, disappointment in his voice. "You pick me up at the old Haida camp." Rifle slung across his back, Gene worked his way over the old log to the other side.

I returned to camp for the boat. For two hours we searched the stream and tide flats. In glum spirits we rowed to the bunkhouse.

By the following morning the stream was again flowing within its banks. Once more we combed the stream and flats. Gulls, ravens, crows, and eagles were enjoying a salmon feast. So were two bears, both good-sized animals but much smaller than the one Gene shot.

Gene's prize had to be somewhere in the deep salt water.

I'm sure the bear would have scored high in the "Boone and Crocket" records. Without that downpour, we could have proved it.

"I'm sorry to lose that one, even though his hide was pretty well beaten up," Gene said. "It's probably the only bear I'll ever shoot. At least I have a broken fang as proof."

6

New Year's Beachcombers

The logs that Leo Saarnok and I delivered to South Bay were scaled (measured to determine the number of board feet of lumber in each log) and paid for. Leo stopped by with the scaler's report and paid us. Gene and I were happy we had gone contract. Our three dollars per thousand board feet amounted to well over two thousand dollars each for two months of work.

"We're going to be in the city for a month or so and need somebody to watch *Islander* and run the engine every week or two," Leo said as we sat around our roaring fireplace. "Insurance is paid up, and the fuel tanks are full. If you want to go beachcombing and pick up a few of our lost logs, you can make some extra dollars."

I had handled *Islander* while we were logging. She was a lovely forty-foot tug less than five years old, in virtually new condition, and her big supercharged Cat diesel had been babied.

"Sounds good to me, Leo. Who do we deliver logs to and how do we split?"

"I've talked to the boss at Crown Zee." Leo pulled a fresh cigar from his shirt pocket. "He'll pay twenty-five dollars a thousand for logs with bark on. No slicks. Too much sand and rocks. You keep half the pay." Leo paused to fire the rum-soaked Crooks. "I'm selling the tug along with my claims and other equipment. Won't get a penny more if the fuel tanks are full, so you might as well use it. Maybe we'll get back some of what we lost when the Indians opened our boomsticks."

For the first time in my life I had grown a beard. It came out gray, even grayer than my hair. Being relatively new in town, I was asked to be Santa Claus at the children's party held at the Airport Hall. I'm not the jolly ho-ho-ho type, but I managed to distribute the gifts and candies without scaring too many toddlers.

Sandspit was nearly dead. Crown Zellerbach's camp closed the week before Christmas. All single loggers and many of the families flew to Vancouver for the holidays. We were glad to be away from the big cities and bright lights and have a quiet time—just the three of us. We wished George and his family could have been there too.

We had our white Christmas. Snow fell on Christmas Eve, clinging to everything. There were three or four inches on the ground and roofs, and the trees carried sparkling loads on every bending branch.

We were still eating turkey on Boxing Day—a new holiday to us. I thought it was appropriately named, for it was also our twenty-fifth wedding anniversary.

On December twenty-ninth, we loaded *Skylark* with provisions, tied her alongside *Islander*, and headed west. A relatively warm southwester was blowing ten to fifteen knots, melting the snow. There were hundreds of scoters and other winter waterfowl on the water, but most sensible humans were enjoying a restful holiday season.

We eyeballed both shores as we passed through the narrows. There were a number of good logs just above the tide line. "Looks like we'll make some easy money," I confidently predicted. Betty and Gene were crowded into *Islander's* small pilot house. Coffee boiled on the oil stove, and a plate of fruitcake sat on the cabin table.

We decided to base our operations in the West Narrows, at Leo's old campsite. He had left a standing boom moored there in the back eddy of a sharp bend. There was plenty of space to tie up the tug, our boat, and the dozen boomsticks we had picked up at South Bay.

The sun peeked through for a few minutes before we moored. "This will be a nice way to spend New Year's," Betty said.

We ate and slept aboard *Skylark*. Our hours of work would depend on two factors: the eight hours of winter daylight and the high tides. Both factors were limiting, and they did not always coincide.

The next forenoon we began beachcombing on the rising tide. I nosed the tug ashore so that Gene could jump off and secure the towline around the log. When Gene signaled, I would throw *Islander* into reverse, increase the RPMs, and back into the flowing tide, rolling the log into the water.

Once afloat, Betty would keep the tug offshore while I shifted the towline aft and took in most of the slack. Then we would head for the bag of boomsticks, open it, and, with a pike pole, shove our log in. Then we would go after another log. We did this for nearly two days before we realized that we were spending all of our time towing logs and opening and closing the bag.

"I can tow logs with *Skylark*," Betty offered.

"Good idea! Gene can drive a dog with a ten-or-fifteen-foot line on it into the small end of each log before we yank it off the beach. Then you catch it and either tow or hold it till we have two or three. When you get back to the bag, just tie them to a boom chain. We'll slip them into the bag when we take the dogs out. We'll try that tomorrow."

"There go our logs!" Gene bellowed. We were towing our last log of the day—and of 1966—to the bag. The tide was ebbing, hurrying our bag of logs out of the narrows and into Skidegate Channel.

"We must have ripped a toggle through one of the sticks. I bet they're all teredo eaten," I said with disgust. "We'll let them go while we tie this one to the standing boom." It was about three o'clock. Dusk would soon overtake us. It was a cold day, and the water was flat and moving fast.

Gene drove a dog into the log and tied it to the standing boom. Then we charged after the bag and nine logs—the meager results of a day-and-a-half's work.

We overtook the bag as it drifted in the wide channel. As we moved alongside it, Gene tied the towline to the ring of a boom chain at the front of our dozen sticks. We had brought the tail end around and made a bag, holding it closed with a short line that we could slip over each new log we shoved into the bag. Gene dropped the eye of the towline over the bitt, and we headed back into the narrows against an outflowing tide. *Islander* slowed as we entered the most restricted portion of the West Narrows. I increased the RPMs to no avail.

Kelp lay flat along the shallow bottom. The outflow's velocity increased, and *Islander* swung like a pendulum as she strained against the tide. The rocky shore was close abreast to port. Black boulders, their worn tops above the swirling water, lay abeam to starboard.

The flow increased for another hour. Our few logs were pressed against the back of the bag, holding two 66-foot boomsticks across the narrow channel. *Islander* was towing a flexible triangle of boomsticks 330 feet on each side and 132 feet across the base. No wonder we weren't moving ahead!

I couldn't turn around in that restricted area. Slowing down and letting the bag pull us out stern first might land us on the beach and damage the screw when the current swept around the point. We couldn't lift the eye of the taut towline over the bitt. And I refused to consider cutting it.

"If you can get back and cut the small line—letting the bag open— the sticks will straighten out and we can pull them," I told Gene. "We'll just have to let the logs go and save the boomsticks." It was dusk, and I couldn't let the bag wash out to sea. I was thankful we didn't have any more logs in the bag.

Gene looped the skiff's bowline around the towline. "I'll just weasel along here till I get to the sticks," Gene said as he picked up a sharp knife.

"Watch out the water doesn't wash you over the logs!" I called from the pilot house.

Gene stepped into the boat and let it slide along the towline. The skiff touched the boomstick. Suddenly, with only a moment's warning, rushing water pressed the boat under the boomstick.

Quick as a cat, Gene leaped onto the stick, the knife tight in his hand, his caulked boots dry. The skiff came up on the inside of the bag, full of water, the oars caught under the seat.

How long could Gene balance on that vibrating log? If he fell . . . .

Betty grabbed a lifejacket, ready to throw it. There was no use in yelling instructions; our words would be drowned by the rumbling diesel and turbulent water.

For a few seconds Gene studied the situation; then he stepped into the water-filled skiff. Its flotation tanks supported his weight. Grasping the bowline, he pulled himself up to the boom chain and, with one fast slash, cut the line. The sticks flowed away in a great arc. Our beachcombed logs rushed seaward. We wouldn't see them again! The boomsticks snapped into a line astern, weaving slightly, like the tail of a kite. For the first time in a half-hour, *Islander* began to move forward—slowly.

It was dark when we finished tying up *Islander* and the boomsticks. "We'll make up the bag tomorrow," I said, grateful that we had lost only a few logs.

Our venison supper was more than a traditional New Year's Eve feast. It was a meal of thanksgiving—thanksgiving for Gene's safety.

On New Year's Day we rigged the bag, making sure it was well secured to the standing boom and shore. Then we tried our idea of letting Betty catch the logs with *Skylark*. It worked. Our production doubled.

Some of the logs we recovered were marked with Leo's stamp. I didn't recognize any of the other brands, but they were legally beachcombed logs. We didn't bother with logs that were less than 350-400 board feet. Some were about 1,000 board feet; a few, as much as 3,000 board feet. Gene was good at guessing their value and often yelled as he signaled me to pull, "There's a fifty-dollar log!"—or whatever value he thought it to be.

Because *Skylark* didn't have the power to pull, or even hold, some of the logs when the tide was running against her, we had to watch the tides closely. At such times, Betty kept our boat in the back eddy of an islet or pocket along the shore, and I would bring the log to her.

If the tide wasn't running too fast, I would pull the log offshore and cast it loose. Betty would run *Skylark* alongside and catch the dogged line with a pike pole. Sometimes our boat and a log would race along side by side as the tide carried them east or west in the riverlike narrows.

A large hemlock of about thirty-five hundred feet—or, as Gene said, "Eighty or ninety dollars in that one"—lay on the narrows' south side. All of its bark was on, and it appeared to be a choice log.

Gene leaped ashore and worked the line under and around the log five times, a good rolling hitch. It should spin across the rocks and into the nearly slack water. I backed offshore, turned *Islander* around, and shifted the eye of the line from bow- to after-towing bitt.

Gene was standing well clear when he signaled. I gunned the supercharged diesel, and *Islander* leaped forward. The log rolled into the water. Momentum carried us halfway across the channel. I turned *Islander* toward the bag, then looked for our log.

It wasn't in sight. Neither was the towline. A half-dozen fast steps, and I was at the stern. My eyes followed the towline into the water until it disappeared fifteen to twenty feet below. "A miserable deadhead!" I bellowed. And Leo's towline was securely tied to it. Gene knew how to tie knots properly.

I let *Islander* swing as the short period of slack tide ended, pulling in on the towline until it was up and down, and then threw a couple of turns around the bitt. We were anchored. If I cut the line, we would have only about twenty-five feet of the heavy one-hundred-foot towline to work with—a loss to Leo and the end of our beachcombing. Gradually I built up speed, slowly dragging and bouncing the water-soaked hemlock over the bottom for nearly a half-mile before the line slipped off and floated to the surface.

We couldn't figure out how that deadhead had come ashore. Since then we have occasionally seen deadheads cast up by the sea's churning action during severe storms.

A big spruce of four thousand to five thousand feet was aground on Downie Island. The water was shallow, so we waited for high tide to go after it. Again *Skylark* was left at the standing boom, and Betty came aboard to help me after we put Gene ashore with the skiff.

Gene had to dig under this log to get the line around and tie a slipknot. The current was not rushing, and I intended to turn around and pull from the stern.

I was watching the current and feeling *Islander's* bow touch gravel. The towline floated nearby, but clear. I threw the tug into reverse and increased speed. Almost instantly there was a solid thunk. In one continuous motion I shoved the throttle to idle and the transmission to neutral. I had a good idea of the stupid trick I had just pulled.

The towline was solidly wrapped around the propeller. The tide was ebbing. Already *Islander* was swinging parallel to the current, and we could hear and feel her touching the loose gravel. I shifted to ahead and turned the screw over. The line didn't unwind.

I'm no Olympic swimmer and even less of a free-diving champion, but I jerked a knife from my belt, stripped, and leaped over the side. The water was cold, but warmer than the air. I dove—or at least tried to. My head and arms were under—I know that—but I couldn't get down to the screw. Cutting the towline at any other place would be an utter waste of effort. The screw had to be cleared. I tried to pull myself down the line and failed. Betty says I never got my feet under water. Teeth chattering and out of breath, I surfaced for the fourth or fifth time. We would sit there till the tide was out for all I could do.

Earlier, while sandblasting *Islander's* bottom, I had noticed her configuration. Although she had been lashed to a dock and held upright, I believed she would list only a few degrees as the water went out underneath her, instead of tipping over and being flooded by the rising tide. But I hated to gamble on it.

Gene was far from eager, but he saw my useless efforts and came aboard to help. He had no trouble getting down and, after what seemed like a long time but could have been three minutes or less, severed the thick line and cleared the screw.

With the bitter end carried free and the short end hauled aboard, I started the diesel, shifted to ahead, threw the rudder hard over, and gunned the engine. Gravel rattled along the keel and spewed astern. After shifting the rudder, I threw the reduction gears into reverse and gunned the engine—saying a fast prayer at the same time. *Islander* gradually slid off the gravel and into deep water.

We ran along the narrows for a few minutes at various speeds, listening for any thumping, feeling for any vibration, and watching for any abnormal temperature readings. All was well. We had been lucky.

"Okay, let's get that log!" I swung the tug around and headed for the beach. Soon it was in the bag, the largest one we had salvaged.

That evening I made a long splice in the towline.

At the end of ten days we had about thirty thousand feet of logs and were thinking about how much we had made. It was clear profit, for all we were putting into this operation was our time and the few gallons of diesel oil *Skylark* burned.

We had collected all the valuable logs around the West Narrows and were ready to tow them through the narrows and begin work in Skidegate Inlet. I checked the chart and tide book; then figured slack tide at the gorge east of Trounce Inlet. We could go through on a flooding tide, towing against a one-or-two-knot current east of the gorge.

We made the bag smaller but couldn't quite double it; we were one or two sticks short of having that extra safety. The towline was tied on and shortened—no more dropping the eye over the bitt. *Islander* was in the lead; Gene and Betty trailed behind in *Skylark* in case any logs slipped out under the sticks.

The egg-shaped tow followed dead astern. We made better speed than I had anticipated. The water in the gorge was flat; there were no whirlpools now. I steered for the center of the narrow, rock-sided channel.

I kept checking ahead and astern. All was well. The bag was entering the gorge. Abruptly, for some inexplicable reason, the bag swung to port, hit a sharp-cornered rock, and ripped the chain out of a stick. Our logs slipped out of the bag before I could stop *Islander*.

There was no place wide enough at that stage of the tide to reverse the course of a single screw tug with a tow. Reconnecting the boomsticks into a bag while drifting in waters that would soon be alive with whirlpools was a job not worth the risk. I increased speed and headed on through the narrows. We had to return the sticks; we didn't have to bring in any logs. I hoped Gene and Betty would be able to catch a few of the larger logs, get dogs into them, and hold on until I returned.

There was a small notch at the east end of the narrows. I shoved the boomsticks ashore, left the rudder amidships and the screw turning over slowly, leaped ashore, tied the sticks to the nearest tree, and climbed back aboard.

A little over fifteen minutes elapsed between the breaking of the bag and *Islander's* return to *Skylark*. Betty and Gene tied our boat alongside and then secured five nice logs to the towing bitt. Our other logs were fanned out, drifting away on the tide. We didn't have more dogs. Whirlpools were forming west of the gorge.

"Let them go!" I yelled. "That's the third escape for some of them."

We were not happy. We had risked our lives and Leo's tug, and we had experienced problems as a result of my inexperience as a beachcomber and as a result of using teredo-eaten boomsticks that should have been sent to the pulp mill months ago.

After picking up the boomsticks, we headed for Alliford Bay and home. A hot shower, a couple nights' sleep in a soft bed, and maybe we would feel ready to try again.

We left *Skylark* at the float when we went out the next week. Betty helped me on the tug. We picked up a few logs every day we worked.

During this time the father of a friend of ours, Shirley Pollard, was visiting her. He lived east of the Rockies and wanted to go out on a boat. A working tug is not the best place to take anyone unused to the sea. He was an active fifty-five or thereabouts, however, and I was talked into taking them beachcombing.

"He can do my work on deck," Betty said, "while Shirley and I hike the beaches."

It was a lovely winter day. The blue sky was alive with pearly cumulus clouds, and tiny waves lapped the shores of the island-studded Skidegate Inlet. Sea ducks drifted along the beaches, and eagles surveyed us from tall snags.

"These are beautiful islands and quite an enjoyable change for me," Shirley's father assured us as we cruised along looking for good logs.

We found a big peeler spruce from Alaska and rolled that one-hundred-dollar bill off the beach. Then we found a smaller log of about a thousand board feet.

Before starting work, I had explained the dangers of being caught in the bight, or loop, of a line. Gene put on a rolling hitch and I dropped the eye over the bitt. Fathoms of towline lay across the stern, ready for running.

"All clear!" I hollered, at the same time checking ahead and astern.

"Okay," Shirley's father replied.

Islander jerked ahead as I hit the throttle. Line leaped and twisted across the stern. For some reason Shirley's father stepped astern; moving line snapped around his leg. The line was nearly run out—one end on the bitt and the other around the heavy log—and his leg was caught in the bight between.

I slammed *Islander* into full astern. We continued forward. All slack came out of the line, and the loop tightened around his leg, jerking him to the deck just as *Islander* stopped.

After determining that he was uninjured—except for his dignity—I helped him up. There were two extremely disturbed men aboard *Islander*. From then on I didn't have to remind him to stay clear of the towline.

During the following days we salvaged a few more logs. Then we took our pitiful little tow to South Bay, where it was scaled, and we were soon paid.

A few weeks later Leo returned, and I told him of some of our misadventures before handing him the full check for the logs.

"We've talked it over and think you should have it all. It's hardly worth dividing. We're satisfied; we had a million dollars' worth of experience—and survived to benefit from it."

Our three weeks of beachcombing had brought a check of $265. There had to be a better way to earn a few dollars.

7

Building the House at Puffin Cove

We wanted to build a tree house like the one in Swiss Family Robinson. Where to build it was the problem. The land around Puffin Cove's beautiful lagoon is uneven, often sloping sharply, and some spots are exposed to wild wind and sea storms. One choice site was atop a steep, upswept sand dune—too unstable and too high to climb often with building materials or even provisions.

Our lease for Puffin Cove could be renewed annually with the Provincial Forestry Department. I didn't intend to haul in cement and pour concrete footings and foundations that would have to be destroyed whenever our lease was canceled—either by the department or by us.

A huge Sitka spruce—gnarled, misshapen, and solitary—stood at the edge of a natural hillside clearing. It was bounded on the south by a modest year-round stream and sheltered on the north by virgin forest and steep mountains. Widespread roots supported a thick bole that rose some eight feet before dividing, one part growing straight as an ordinary tree some eighteen inches in diameter, the others extending out as massive arms paralleling the ground before returning to the vertical. We studied the tree from every angle.

"That tree has lots of possibilities," Gene said, "if we can only figure them out."

"Timbers extended from the lower arm to the slope could form a foundation," I suggested. This plan would simplify building. The upper arm, with its two fifteen-inch vertical trunks, could easily support a comfortable living room, allowing us to construct a modern, split-level home.

The location gave an excellent view of the lagoon and was near our freshwater supply. In addition, we could watch the deer browse in the glade as they passed to and from the beach. We had often seen them suddenly appear in the clearing, pause a few minutes while making a safety check, and then amble onto the beach in search of freshly washed-in kelp.

"Those limbs were bigger than lots of trees Dad and I used to cut," I told Betty and Gene after sawing off the upper part of two large limbs. The tree was sound, though an old fire-blackened scar might have been the explanation for its unique shape.

"I want to see the ocean," I said. We had had an ocean view in California, where there was little to see except a few rows of lazy surf and lingering sunsets that got redder each year as the smog increased. "Here the sea's alive. It's always changing; it's violent and wild. We'll miss that from a tree house."

"I don't think you'll get enough sunshine here," said Gene, his courses in architecture coming to our aid again. "Build where you'll get maximum sunlight. Winter days are short enough without living in the shade of trees or mountains."

So we considered a rocky point near the center of the crescent-shaped lagoon. It was covered with twisted, stunted pines and cedars, reminding us of the much-photographed peninsula of Monterey, California. Those tortured trees were evidence of the winds, which reached seventy-five knots or more. Could we build a cabin strong enough?

Because of foundation problems, we had discarded the idea of building on a rounded rock offering a fine view through the entrance. Now we reconsidered. Six spruce trees grew here, their roots spread wide, gripping into crevices in the cracked and eroded granite.

"We could cut some of the trees and build on their stumps," I said.

"There's no way any combination of stumps will form a rectangle," Betty objected.

"Who, aside from bureaucracy-bound building inspectors, claim a house has to be made with each corner at a ninety-degree angle?"

"Your idea sounds good to me," Gene said, "and you'll have a view all the way to Japan." It was a bright, sunny place.

The tree house idea was out. It had been a picturesque dream.

One of the six trees was hollow. We felled it out of the way. Next was a lofty, high-limbed tree over thirty-six inches in diameter. I dropped it across a narrow defile and onto a low, salal-covered rock. "If you'll limb that, Gene, we can use it for a footbridge," Betty said.

Two more trees were cut, and two were left standing. We had three solid stumps to build on. They would determine the size of our cabin.

"We'll use a piling for the fourth corner," I said.

The cabin would have two square corners at the end next to a steep bank that rose about fifteen feet before leveling off into the forest. The angled ends faced seaward.

Because of the lagoon's restricted entrance and riverlike outward flow, few logs drifted in. Outside, on the open coast, was a long rocky beach covered with logs, lumber, and other drift, accumulated since logging began on Vancouver Island, in Alaska, and in the Queen Charlottes. Here we found heavy timbers of sufficient length for our stump-supported foundation, plus a creosoted six-by-twelve that we used as a diagonal support for floor joists.

With fulcrums and brute force, the three of us worked these treasures across rounded boulders until they lay just above the tide line. Because of the crashing waves and grinding rocks, we had to yell at each other. "Now I know why all these rocks are smooth," Betty shouted. Powerful incoming waves rolled the rocks landward; retreating waves dragged them back.

We would have to wait for the sea to quiet before rolling our timbers into the water.

"Let's see what's behind our lagoon," Betty suggested the next day, "since it's still too rough to get those timbers. I'll pack a lunch."

Behind our lagoon, with its five separate beaches, was another lagoon, its entrance blocked by three pointed boulders staggered between the walls of a gorge. As a result, during the middle of flood or ebb tide, a skookumchuck—fast or strong water—scoured the sand, creating a pool.

"That hole looks deep enough to hold *Skylark*," I said as we went along a sheer cliff. "I'll have to make a good float first. One with a log roller so it won't hang up on any of the rough points as the tide rises and falls under it."

At high tide we took Betty's dugout into the second lagoon and rowed around its edges, which steeply rose to the south, climbed in a series of low steps to a hill on the north, and were covered with dwarf pines and cedars. To the east, a short stream burbled and tumbled over slippery black rocks as it rushed from a lake ringed with waterlilies. A belted kingfisher dove from an overhanging branch, and ducks paddled toward the opposite shore. Fog crept along the cloud-shadowed mountainside.

Eroded and glaciated mountains sparsely covered with

stunted trees and clumps of grass rose on the lake's north side. A lively, translucent stream splashed into the lake from rock-rimmed sluiceways. Falls tumbled from a large mountain lake some fifteen hundred feet above the sea that drained an area of perhaps ten square miles.

A red-tailed hawk screamed as it drifted high overhead. "Not many birds here," Betty observed. "I've seen only the hawk and one song sparrow."

Three deer, roused from an afternoon nap, stood up, eyed us curiously, and ambled off. Tracks of a large bear marked the mud near the stream. "A good-sized one," I told Betty, "but nowhere near the size of the one Gene shot."

"Tide's coming in and the sea's quiet," I announced to my crew next day. "Let's get those timbers into the chuck."

As the tide lifted and jostled the long timbers, we shoved out with pike poles, pushing each reluctant piece through the small waves, keeping them offshore until the tide turned and pulled them seaward.

"Gene, you stay outside the kelp with *Skylark* while Betty and I work near shore with the skiff. We'll round them up in nothing flat."

Betty and I dropped into the skiff, and I yanked the outboard into life. We shoved the timbers into deep water one at a time, drove a dog in, and towed them through the kelp to the waiting *Skylark*. Slowly, *Skylark* towed the six obstinate pieces into the lagoon.

With blocks and tackle and a come-along rigged to the standing trees, we laboriously dragged and hoisted the twelve-by-twelve spruce timbers to our building site about fifteen feet above the high-water mark.

"There must be an easier way," Gene said, wiping the sweat from his face, "but I don't know how."

"Not much progress," I agreed, "since the pyramids were built over four thousand years ago."

We leveled the stumps and notched them to receive the

timbers. Then we drilled the timbers to take sharpened iron rods, 20 inches long and ¾ inch in diameter, which we drove like supernails deep into the stumps.

The summer days were long and full. We had light from before 5:00 a.m. until after 10:00 p.m.—longer working hours than we could physically take. Betty dug to bedrock for the fourth corner post. We mixed a little concrete and set up the four-foot piling. Our foundation was completed. It stood four to six feet above the uneven rock.

"Grab the end of the tape, Gene, and we'll see what size this thing will be." Betty made a rough sketch as I called out the figures. "Twelve feet wide. Eighteen feet long on the south side. Sixteen feet on the north. It's no castle, but big enough."

There was little more we could do without lumber, so we boarded *Skylark* and headed for Sandspit, beachcombing along the way.

Rough-cut cedar would be adequate for all the framing as well as for the trim. The island's only sawmill was in Queen Charlotte City. I phoned Al Porter, the owner. "Got lots of orders, and my helper quit yesterday. And no prospects for another. I'm just about shut down." After a long pause, Al added, "Might be able to help you out if you or your boy could give me a hand."

Gene volunteered. I couldn't work because Betty and I were committed to taking scientists from Vancouver and Ottawa on a two-week charter along the west and north coasts of Graham Island.

Helping to saw lumber for our cabin was Gene's farewell present to us before he returned to California to answer his draft call and enter the U.S. Army for a year in Viet Nam as a communications specialist. I suspect that working in the sawmill was the last thing Gene ever volunteered for.

Betty and I went to the bay-side mill and loaded *Skylark* at high tide. I carried the wood to the water's edge and shoved it out. Betty snagged it with a short pike pole and hauled it aboard. It took two days and three trips to get it across Skidegate Inlet to Alliford Bay and truck it home. The waters were quiet, and we loaded heavily. On the last trip we hit strong crosscurrents and *Skylark,* overloaded and top-heavy, rolled nastily. Some two-by-eights tumbled off, taking the port running light with them.

In Sandspit I used my electric saw to cut joists and studs to length and then to notch and angle the rafters. Our order of plywood, insulation, and nails finally arrived. During the spring we had split and bundled shakes for the cabin roof. We traded a few large glass balls for wood-framed windows. We had everything we needed to complete construction—but it was all in Sandspit, over one hundred miles by water from Puffin Cove.

"It'll take at least four trips," I told Betty, "a month or six weeks—depending on the weather—to get all this stuff to Puffin Cove. By then summer will be over and fall gales may take all the fun out of building."

Skylark was partially loaded when friends arrived in Sandspit with their fifty-foot boat, *Sundown*, and, after telling us they were going through the narrows and down the west coast, asked if there was anything they could do for us. Was there!

They were an answer to prayer. That evening we trucked our building supplies to *Sundown* and loaded her. A few days later we met outside Puffin Cove and unloaded. Thanks to that helpful family, we were able to begin construction immediately.

The next morning dawned bright and clear. Betty and I began work early. By dark the joists were nailed into place, cross-braced, and ready for the subflooring—at the cost of only one bashed thumb. By the following noon the subflooring was on. We laid out the studs and knocked together the framework for the long side. Once it was in place, we started on the other three sides. Each day was full and satisfying and brought our cabin nearer completion.

During our trips in 1954 and 1955 we had found cabins ruined because a door was open. "I've got the answer to that problem," I told Betty one morning when we slowed down for coffee. "We'll enter through the floor. I'll make a trapdoor." I figured if it was left open it wouldn't hurt; in fact, it might be beneficial, since circulating air would keep the cabin dry and free of mildew.

Of course a trapdoor meant lost floor space in an already small room, but we would gain wall space. And the door wouldn't be locked. Our food- and wood-stocked cabin might save some shipwrecked mariner or downed pilot. Besides, I didn't want to have to repair a door smashed by anyone breaking in. Locks only keep out honest people.

Occasionally we would take an hour or so off to hike through the forest and along the outer beach. "Go ahead, Betty," I said one sunny morning when Betty suggested a walk to "see what's drifted in." "I'll stay and get these window frames in."

I had already cut out and framed the trapdoor and was happily nailing in window frames. Without thinking, I stepped back to admire the view—and fell through the trapdoor opening onto a rotting log. During the four-foot fall I turned slightly and landed on my right kidney and back. My head hit the ground. I was stunned. I don't recall the view through the window, but I saw stars through the trapdoor opening.

Then the pain! Was my back broken? I tried to wiggle my foot and was rewarded by seeing it respond. "You're a lucky boy, Neil," I said aloud. By the time Betty returned, I was limping slowly about—and the trapdoor was covered with a thick piece of plywood.

Whenever we wanted fresh fish we would take the skiff to the outer bay. In a few minutes of jigging we usually caught a nice lingcod or halibut. One day we went three miles south to another bay and shot a deer.

"Let's not shoot anything in Puffin Cove," Betty had said

when we started building. "The animals and birds here will be our friends and neighbors."

"I'll buy that." I have been tempted a couple times when, after weeks of nothing but fish and canned meat for the main course, a nice fat buck ambled past the cabin.

Before mid-September, and without any problems more serious than slivers or black thumbnails, we had the cabin up, sided, and roofed; the windows in; and the Yukon chimney installed. Whenever it rained we laid flooring, put in spun-glass insulation, nailed on interior panel boards, fitted molding around the windows, and made a large trapdoor and set of steps. The final task was to line the floor and wall of the oblique corner with bricks.

That was where the wood stove was to be placed—if the Vancouver dealer ever got around to shipping it. It should have arrived in Sandspit long before we left.

Already there were mornings when we would have appreciated a fire while we worked. And it would have been much easier for Betty to cook in the cabin instead of on the boat.

We hated to do it, but soon it was time to leave Puffin Cove. Betty wanted to see EXPO '67, so we were off to Montreal.

The following spring we headed to Puffin Cove with materials to build a bathhouse. An extra-long, old-fashioned iron tub lay across *Skylark's* stern.

"We're spending all our time at sea," Betty complained when we immediately headed back to Sandspit to pick up two galvanized barrels and pipe to make the bathhouse stove and water tank, "and don't have time to enjoy Puffin Cove."

Our friend, Emil Larka, helped make the drum stove and plumbing hookup. Just to make sure it was done right, we talked Emil into going with us and returning to Sandspit along the east coast.

The trip from Sandspit to Tasu was rough. April storms

kept us in Tasu Sound for nearly a week. Finally the storms calmed to a twenty-five-knot southeaster, and we battled our way to Puffin Cove. Emil had fished the northern lakes and had been skipper of a boat in Lake Superior, so he was used to foul weather. But none of us enjoyed it.

"A bear cub could have done better!" was Emil's considered opinion of my plywood bathhouse.

It wasn't tight enough for a good steam room. Wind blew in from under the plank floor. Emil stuffed moss around the windows and the other wide cracks created by my chain-saw carpentry. We put a metal form around the fire barrel and then filled it with small rocks until only a hole for the stovepipe remained.

The water barrel was filled by a hose from the stream. A bucket of fine gravel was tossed into the bottom of the stove, and then a fire was lit. Three hours later boiling water rumbled in the pipes, and the building was hot.

"Just sprinkle hot water on those rocks and you'll have a dry-steam sauna," Emil said, grabbing his towel.

A half-hour later Emil returned. "Nothing but wet steam! All the heat goes out through the plywood and cracks," he growled. "Don't tell anyone I had anything to do with this abortion."

But Betty and I were pleased with our bathhouse and sauna. It completed everything we required for a simple life.

During the following years we made changes in and additions to the cabin. We put a porch on the front that sheltered the excavated space under the cabin, where we store some of our beachcombings. We replaced small single windows with larger storm windows. And we installed a window beside our bed so that Betty can read an extra hour or so morning and evening without the gas lantern.

We are proud of our snug little cabin, although we agree that *House Beautiful* is unlikely to feature it as House of the Month. But, as Betty said, "This is what I've always dreamed of and wanted!"

A fall gale churns up the North Pacific outside Puffin Cove.

Betty Carey and her companion Iva

Betty Carey climbs 400 steps to the top of St. James Island, where three
persons maintain a meteorological station.

Nailing in floor joists for the cabin at Puffin Cove.

← Heavy construction lumber 4x4s and 12x12s washed ashore on Puffin Cove's be during a March gale. The Careys salvaged some of th but most was soon broken, cracked, or had corners rounded by subsequent gale and was soon useful only as firewood.

Neil Carey unloading a boa load of 4x4s brought into th lagoon from the outer beach This lumber was lost from freighter during a severe winter storm, cast on the rocky shore and soon batter and cracked until usable onl for firewood. →

Six-foot-two logger Leo Saarnok lies atop the stump of a giant spruce and reaches only halfway across.

Faller Ralph Emde uses a springboard to stand on as he prepares to drop this giant spruce for Leo Saarnok on Graham Island timber claim.

summer day at Puffin Cove.

← Aerial view of Puffin Cove at low tide.

Winter at Puffin Cove. This much snow is rare and seldom lasts as much as ten days.

Puffin Cove. Betty Carey waves a message bottle that she will toss into the ocean. Replies came from Alaska, Oregon, and British Columbia, and there was one from the Suez Canal from a sailor who had picked the bottle up in Tasu.

Carey with life rings
chcombed on the west
st of Moresby Island.

A pair of 2x4s, an inflatable fishing float, and a few plastic floats were all Betty
Carey gleaned while beachcombing Cape Freeman this time.

Japanese glass balls found on Graham Island.

il Carey with plastic floats beachcombed at McLean Fraser Point.

Beachcombing.

Oriental pot dug up at abandoned whaling station at Rose Harbor.

←
This Japanese mine, a reminder of World War II, drifted across the Pacific and was rolled across the reef and logs of Hunter Point without detonating. The chemically activated horns have been battered nearly flat. The explosive has been dissolved.

Betty Carey rowing her dugout away from Ninstints Village on Anthony Island. Ninstints had, and still has, the best collection of Haida totems.

← Part of a carved Haida bowl, and high-grade copper ore salvaged from the wrecked *Kennecott*, found by the Careys during an April cruise.

A leaning mortuary pole at Ninstints. →

A fine example of Haida art, this pole stands at Ninstints Village. How much longer will this unique mortuary pole remain?

With each visit to Ninstints, Neil sees fewer standing totems. Here feels the shallow scallop marks le the skillful carver of this unusual

After enjoying the haunting beauty of abandoned Ninstints Village, Betty Carey paddles away in her Indian dugout canoe.

The Careys in *Skylark* passing Hippa Fangs near Hippa Island during an April cruise. (Photo by Dr. P. Mylechreest.)

ylark, the Careys' 26-foot converted lifeboat, moored in Puffin Cove.

Neil and Betty Carey with a glass ball beachcombed while stormbound on the west coast of Graham Island. (Photo by Dr. P. Mylechreest)

Preparing Betty's dugout for her trip from Prince Rupert to Anacortes, Washington.

Captain Fred Hargraves of the Forestry Vessel *Hecate Ranger* plotting the course from Sandspit to Prince Rupert.

All loaded and ready to go.

Betty Carey and Ivan passing the Northland freighter, *Skeena Prince*, in Cumshewa Inlet.

Neil Carey with a 13-pound coho caught in front of the Sandspit home.

Caught in the open bay at Wells Cove by a sudden gale, *Skylark* was taken upstream at high tide and secured to the trees by Neil Carey.

Neil Carey scraping gooseneck barnacles from a freshly washed ashore Japanese hatch board. These hatch boards, lost from fishing vessels or coastal merchant ships, are made of four to six squared pieces of Port Orford cedar, grown in Japan, and can be made into attractive coffee tables or benches.

A load of stove wood for use in *Skylark*.

A few of the Careys' beachcombed trophies. The jawbones are from a 50-foot sperm whale, complete with teeth; the vertebra is from a 75-80-foot whale; and the glass float is from a Japanese fishing vessel.

his 30-pound halibut will provide many tasty meals for the Careys. If the sea is iet, it is possible for them to catch halibut, cod, or red snapper nearly ytime.

Lashing the anchor from the S.S. *Florence* to logs at Carew Bay before towing to Sandspit.

Neil Carey with wreckage from the S.S. *Florence* on Kindakun P

Part of anchor chain from the S.S. *Florence* wrecked on the rocks of Kindakun Point.

The Careys look from a basalt plug toward the wreck of the U.S.A.T.S. *Clarksdale Victory* on Hippa Island. Forty-nine of the 53-man crew died when a November gale drove the ship onto this reef. (Photo by Dr. P. Mylechreest.)

The dangling anchor chain of the U.S.A.T.S. *Clarksdale Victory* tells of an attempt to hold the ship off the reef at Hippa Island. The port anchor hangs above Betty Carey as she explores the wreck and reef.

Bow section of the U.S.A.T.S. *Clarksdale Victory* on the reef at Hippa Island.
Betty Carey climbs out of number one hold.

A winter sunset seen from the cabin at Puffin Cove.

Betty Carey rowing through the narrow entrance to Puffin Cove. The cabi
is in the background and provides a view of the open ocean.→

8

Winter Cruise

Our stone fireplace is a hungry brute. Its mouth is forty-two inches wide. I was splitting frosted lengths of green spruce to feed it when Bill, a big logger, drove into the yard.

"Happy New Year!" I called as he opened his pickup door.

"Same to you!" My twelve-pound maul slammed onto the wedge again and the knotty block reluctantly cracked open.

"Hear you're going out to the west coast," Bill said, turning up his collar.

I nodded, upended another chunk, and tapped the wedge into position.

"Anybody's a fool to go out there this time of year." He waved his brawny arm toward the snow-laden Slatechuck Mountains, now aglow with the pinkish cast of a late-rising winter sun. Billowing clouds balanced on the ridges. A bald eagle winged low overhead and landed on the bottom branch of a spruce beside the bay.

"Ever been to the west coast in winter?" I picked up a heavy chunk of wood and we went inside for coffee.

"Nothin' but wild, killer storms out there," came Bill's evasive answer.

I pressed my question after shoving the chunk into the base of the roaring fire.

"Well, no . . . but I've sure heard plenty."

"Ever been out there in summer?" I filled the cups.

"Can't say I have," the young logger admitted with a wry grin. "But for sure every year some guy loses his boat or life out there. Out where there's no help. That's why the wife and I haven't made it—yet."

"Right. And just last month a ten-thousand-ton ship went down with all hands less than four hundred miles off the coast. Same thing a year ago, just before Christmas. And that captain had his wife along too."

The hearth is cantilevered at chair height. We were already too warm, so we slid to opposite ends of the fireplace. "Those actic highs often lie over the mainland and the Charlottes in winter, giving us these cold, clear days," I went on. "The winds, if any, blow from north or northeast, flattening the ocean on the west coast—the islands act as a massive breakwater. The Pacific can be almost as calm as a millpond."

"Bet it's colder than a mother-in-law's welcome!" he grinned. Then he gulped another mouthful of hot coffee.

"Almost," I laughed. "But it's not as cold as here in Sandspit. And at Puffin Cove we don't have so large a place to heat. So there's less wood to cut and split."

Bill left unconvinced.

The second week of the new year was here before *Skylark* was fueled and loaded. The arctic high had given us cold, sunny days and calm seas since before Christmas. How much longer would the weather hold?

At high slack water we cast off from the float in Alliford

Bay, site of an abandoned World War II RCAF base. Ice lay in sparkling, cracked sheets, chipping paint from *Skylark's* metal hull. "I can't stand that grinding," Betty said, coming up on deck.

There were no other boats in sight. They had been hauled out of the water after coho fishing ended in October. Gray clouds loaded with snow moved along the low mountains of Graham Island. Moresby's mountains wore a new cloak of snow down to the thousand-foot level.

In Skidegate Narrows long leaves of bullwhip kelp streamed from baseball-size floating heads, tugging at hold-fasts as the ebbing tide flowed westward. (Tides on the east side of the Charlottes sometimes attain heights of twenty-six feet; those on the west, only fourteen feet. This difference in head causes the tidal streams to flow at up to seven knots.) The narrows, filled with this spring tide, appeared wide and straight. In reality, the dredged channel is sinuous and narrow.

Skylark rushed through the gorge at ten to twelve knots. Trees overlapped this sixty-yard-wide gut, their lower branches a uniform height, growth killed by the salt water. Many whirlpools formed, dissipated, and formed again in that rushing, turbulent water, thrusting fish to the surface and pulling branches, chunks of wood, and other debris below, only to be spewed forth a few yards away.

Suddenly an eagle flashed past my head, talons open and pushed forward, great wings spread wide to break its speed. With intuitive precision it snatched up a flopping twelve-inch fish and flew off, its wings never touching the water.

Logging scars in various stages of healing marked Graham, Moresby, and Chaatl islands along Skidegate Channel. The water was as flat as a mirror. Dusk fell at 3:30 p.m. "Won't have time to reach Dawson Harbour," I said, "so we'll go into Armentieres Channel for the night."

It was dark when I dropped the anchor near the channel's head. A minute later I hauled it up; I had missed the steeply shelving bottom. "You've been ashore too long," I told myself.

Canoe Pass, between Armentieres and Buck channels, was already dry, and the tide had another two hours to run out. The pass is a mile-long S-shaped waterway separating Chaatl and Moresby islands. Only the first two hundred yards are tricky, with barely enough water at high tide for *Skylark*. At 1:30 a.m. we could go through on the last of the flood. Going through the pass would save nearly an hour and half of travel. With the last light in the evening sky, I oriented myself, picking out three peaks.

"It'll have to be snowing hard or blacker than coal," I told Betty as we sat in the warm cabin having a light supper, "to keep us from getting through Canoe Pass."

I awakened and shut off the alarm before it rang. No need to disturb Betty. Stars winked through thin clouds. The moon was full and golden bright, ringed with a cold halo.

"An easy fifteen-minute trip through the pass; then back to bed," I promised myself.

Skylark hugged the upswept southeastern shore of Chaatl. We were through the shallowest part. One more hazard: a large rock in the center of the channel. "Will it show or be covered?" The night binoculars caught it—a low, black blob rising a few inches above black water. Ahead, a wide path of scintillating, quicksilvery sea opened, beckoning. Hypnotized by its bright beauty, I steered along the path and failed to anchor.

Fresh, lustrous snow dusted the trees and bare rocks above the five-hundred-foot level. Frost sparkled on everything below. *Skylark's* cabin top and two boats were covered with a half-inch coat of radiant hoarfrost. I was warmly dressed and comfortable—so long as there was no wind.

The ebbing tide hurried us seaward on that moonlit ribbon of liquid silver. On each side dark shores rose steeply, becoming snow-covered hillsides stretching to meet the luminous sky. A gaggle of geese rose from near the southern shore, complaining noisily at being disturbed. "Snow geese," I whispered as they drifted into the mountain's shadow before splashing down, creating tiny white wakes.

Ahead, a small, unnamed bay offered a quiet anchorage. But the boat was riding nicely and making good speed, and I couldn't resist the urge to go on.

The frosty gravel shore of abandoned Chaatl Village shimmered, and a lone totem pole loomed from the surrounding trees. I imagined smoke rising from longhouses and dugout canoes lying on the coarse beach, high above the tide line. The unmistakable odor of wood smoke drifted past. Was this Haida village, derelict for over three-quarters of a century, now inhabited?

No. Enough dreaming at the helm. The burning spruce was in our own stove. It reminded me to go below and tend the fire.

"Are you warm and comfortable?"

Betty awakened enough to mumble yes.

"The sea's flat. We'll go on to Kaisun."

"Good." And Betty was asleep.

Gentle waves lapped at the black headlands of Buck Channel, running unseen up rocks and cascading into snowy falls. *Skylark's* bow rose and dipped sleepily, responding to the North Pacific's rhythm. The moonlit path continued westward, toward the Orient. *Skylark* turned south. The moon and stars illuminated three large offshore rocks rising only a few feet above the water, and Buck Point's jagged silhouette slid into view.

The moon's halo disappeared about 2:30 a.m. Low, broken clouds loomed to the west. Buck Point was astern, and there was nothing to worry about except the threat of deadheads—those water-soaked logs, often floating vertically with just a tip above the surface, sinking for who knows how far and then shooting upward, perhaps into the bottom of some unwary mariner's craft.

What were the odds for avoiding any deadheads? Certainly better than for avoiding a wreck on the Hollywood Freeway, which I had driven into Los Angeles hundreds of times. "It's prettier here too," I reminded myself. "But there's no place along here to stop for a morning cup of coffee and a pair of dunking doughnuts."

In Buck Channel I had seen drifting logs covered with hoarfrost, and I expected to find the same here. Then, north of Kitgoro Inlet, I spotted a rime-topped deadhead. The odds were in our favor.

The precipitous mountain dominating the coast near Kitgoro was luminous with snow. It would be easy to slip into the tiny inlet and anchor. Clouds were building, and the moon was setting, meeting each other halfway.

Even with the binoculars I could not locate the red buoy marking the wreck of a small tug that had been lost in ninety feet of water the previous February, carrying a father and son whom we knew. We had been away at the time of the search. In May we spent three days in the area looking for any sign that they might have reached shore. Betty investigated a large cave that the searchers had not known about. As Bill, the logger, had said, "Every year some guy loses his boat or life out there."

The moon played hide-and-seek behind ragged clouds. The reef south of Kitgoro was not breaking; the sea was too quiet for that. "Probably sliding across like an oily slick," I told myself, steering *Skylark* another half-mile offshore, just to be safe.

Would the setting moon still be uncovered when we passed between the rocks guarding Kaisun Harbour? Another fifteen or twenty minutes would tell. It was going to be close.

A few of the islands speckling Englefield Bay loomed into view. *Skylark* turned toward a slot only slighter lighter than its surroundings—the western opening to Kaisun. For an instant the moonlight brightened, illuminating our destination. Then it dimmed as a checkerboard of clouds played across the sky.

I slipped *Skylark* between jutting rocks and into the flat

harbor, where frost-covered drift logs lay like white chalk marks on a blackboard sea.

For a few minutes moonlight laved the single standing mortuary pole of abandoned Kaisun Village. Weathered and worn, it leaned like an exhausted soldier. The A of a recent landslide streaked through the village site.

Skylark's anchor hit bottom at 4:30 a.m. She rolled gently in this restless harbor. So far, this was one of our smoothest and most beautiful trips. "Hope we reach Puffin Cove before the weather changes," I muttered, examining the sky before I went below.

Dawn arrived cold and too soon. I snuggled down in the warm sleeping bag and dozed, lulled by *Skylark's* slow roll.

Our supply of stove wood was nearly exhausted. As always, Kaisun's beaches were littered with drift logs. A straight, twelve-inch spruce log lay near the water. Betty landed our skiff nearby and beachcombed while I sawed and split a boatload of wood.

"Not much on this beach," Betty said, holding a grape-fruit-size glass ball, "but it's worth climbing over the frosty logs."

In the unflattering light of day the old Haida pole lost much of its beauty and mystery. It was little better than a decaying snag.

Back in the boat, there was only the metallic click of engaging contacts when I pushed the starter button. I checked. All seemed okay. Same results on the second try. Maybe we were foolish to be out there at that time of year with little chance of seeing anyone for weeks or even months.

The starter was not a necessity, just a luxury. We had insisted on an engine that could be started by hand, and that precaution now paid off.

The engine was cold. I was soon sweating. Then it coughed, hacked, and finally fired. "At least the battery's charging," I told Betty. "We can use the lights. I'll just have to crank till the starter's fixed."

Skylark nosed through a cleft in the rocks and into Englefield Bay—only an open roadstead—dotted with islands, islets, and rocks. The sea was calm; the sky, clear; and the temperature; low. The sun provided better illumination than the moon but little more warmth.

Was that spray from a breaking wave? I watched with the binoculars until I was sure. "Thar she blows!" Betty was on deck in seconds. Sighting a whale was becoming a rare event.

"There, just this side of Lihou Island," I said, pointing. "Saw it blow three or four times. Must be feeding." As it came toward us we saw the distinctive forward-angling spout of a sperm whale. Next to it was the smaller spout of a calf. Swimming just beneath the surface, neither broached or sounded. Water slicked as it slid along their rough, dark backs.

Betty smiled. "I always like to know they're around."

We approached Cape Henry, a place of vertical headlands and off-lying rocks. Sometimes we had fought around it; other times we had been turned back. Now it was quiet.

"How about taking over for a while. I'm tired."

Betty knew the coast as well as I did, if not better, and could be counted on to stay in the "rut."

"Neil." Betty poked her head into the cabin. "Look at this!" I checked my watch. I had had about an hour of sleep.

I stepped out of the cabin and noticed the land was astern. It should have been on our port beam. Betty pointed at something in the water. "Could that be part of a boat?"

Something jabbed skyward; then slowly sank. In seconds it gradually rose until some five feet of round, tapered wood protruded. It did look like a mast. Could it be the sailboat that had been lost in the North Pacific more than two months earlier? It repeatedly made the news because the skipper had had an all-female crew. I watched through the binoculars. "Nope. Just another miserable deadhead. Glad we didn't hit it. It would be like a needle in a balloon!"

The last of the tide ebbing out of Tasu Sound met us as we

turned into the "gap." Water here is deep and at times unpredictable. Tide, wind, and ocean swells sometimes combine to make it a witch's cauldron. A large U.S. tuna boat lay below us. Overloaded, it had swamped and sunk in the turbulent entrance—a half-mile from the safety of calm waters. Today it was quiet. We could have nosed up to the rocks on either side and collected starfish hanging there. In the past, however, we have come in from a calm sea and run into berserk local winds whipping the sound into a white-topped boil racing out the gap.

Approaching the mine complex, we sighted a circling Trans-Provincial Beaver. It angled down for a landing near the ship loading dock. "Bet it's frozen over in Hunger Harbour," Betty said. The amphibian gunned its way up the beach, and a van was soon alongside, picking up and discharging passengers and freight.

The open pit mine was blanketed with snow. The mountains were cold and forbidding. Bright lights in the mine office and mill and in the colorfully painted homes were warm and inviting. Although it is a company town, Tasu is modern and attractive. Home for nearly four hundred people, Tasu has large bunkhouses and a capacious mess hall; a store; a post office; a movie room; a recreation building with pool, indoor courts, library, sauna, and a full-time recreation director; and three-teacher school.

Rounding Gowing Island—now attached to Moresby Island by a wide causeway made from the overburden from the mine site—*Skylark* ran into patches of broken ice about two inches thick. We followed a path broken by a RIVTOW tug, now tying up, and we moored to the aircraft float.

"I'll run up and get tickets for dinner," Betty said, while I secured the stern line. "See you in the mess hall."

The food in any camp is excellent—it has to be if the crew is to be retained—varied, and inexpensive. For the past eighteen months it had been superior because of Kurt, the

German chef. Trained in Europe, he had cooked on cruise ships and in luxury hotels. His cooking was superb.

This was Saturday night—steak night. "How do you want it cooked?"

"Blood rare."

"How many?"

That took a moment's thought. "Two, please."

I once saw a ballooning trencherman take five, and I have been told of men who surpassed that—without so much as a discreet belch.

The mess hall is a miniature United Nations, except there is more harmony here. We would always meet men from faraway places, and it was always a pleasure to be able to say: "Yes, we've been to your country, and we enjoyed it." That night we met a Spaniard and a Pakistani, but we hadn't been to either of those countries.

It might be a month or six weeks before we returned for mail and supplies, so together we went through the co-op store, filling shopping carts with supplies for two months. There were already a few cases of tinned food aboard. We half-filled one cart with fresh fruit and vegetables. Fresh venison and fish we could get near Puffin Cove.

After posting letters, making phone calls to parents and sons, and catching a movie, we were ready to shove off. The weather was holding, with warnings for northerly or north-easterly gales. Either would bring cold winds to maintain a calm sea along the west coast, except as we passed the gusting mouths of inlets. I moved *Skylark* to a more exposed float, where there was less chance of being nipped in the ice.

We awakened to find everything covered with an eight-inch blanket of snow. We were surrounded by ice, which I could break with a pike pole.

With sunrise a half-hour away, we cast off. *Skylark's* sharp bow broke through new ice an inch thick. "Sounds like a dozen boys pounding on a metal drum," Betty said as she slipped into a heavy coat and came on deck to stand beside me.

We glanced back at the town. The sky glowed pink, lights shone through decorated windows, and each street light wore a halo—a classic Christmas card scene.

The ocean was calm. Shortly after noon *Skylark* rounded the 490-foot islet outside Puffin Cove and entered the open bay. Fresh drift was scattered over our 'lumberyard beach." We would use some of it for firewood and some for building material. "If the sea's calm tomorrow, we can roll a few logs in and tow them inside the lagoon," I said.

The tide was high enough to enter, and we were once more safely inside the quiet waters of Puffin Cove. We felt happy with life.

Would the seals, otters, deer, Canada geese, bald eagles, ravens, and smaller birds be here to welcome us? We knew the white-footed mice would be.

I wished that Bill, the big logger, could have made this trip and seen the North Pacific millpond.

9

Salmon Patrol

For two months we had been traveling around Moresby Island, starting with the east coast. Now, in late July, we were working our way north, up Moresby's west coast. During the past three weeks, we hadn't seen another boat or an aircraft. Only our radio assured us we were not the last people on earth.

Skylark was nearly loaded with glass balls, plastic floats, life rings, and, best of all, the lower jaw of a fifty-foot sperm whale—complete with teeth. We had also found the skull—about the size and shape of a Volkswagen bug—but we couldn't move it. Fortunately. The jaws smelled bad enough. The lingering odor penetrated everything on the boat.

"I can even taste it," I told Betty one morning at breakfast. But we were determined to have those rare jaws and teeth no matter how they smelled—or how we smelled.

"I can't be sure whether the whale died of old age or was harpooned," I said to Betty as we rolled up the coast. "The teeth are good and the backbone was broken, so I'm guessing it was killed by a whaler." I remembered the one I saw shot through the backbone with a harpoon, which had exploded and blown itself out of the whale.

We were on the way to Sandspit to unload before continuing up Graham Island, and we stopped at Tasu to pick up fresh food and have our mail flown in. Maybe that was a mistake. The skipper of the fisheries patrol boat was having trouble with a leaky stern tube. After seeing us, he phoned the Queen Charlotte City office and suggested we take over his job.

The evening after leaving Tasu we anchored in Security Cove. The *Sooke Post* soon hove around the point, and Captain Ken Harley brought his Fisheries Patrol Vessel alongside. Ken and his crew were often the only people we saw along the Charlottes' west coast, and we were always glad to visit.

"Good collection of bones and teeth you've got there," Ken called out, ignoring their smell. "Come aboard for coffee and cake."

Then he offered us a charter. Whether we took it or not, the boat would have to be unloaded and cleaned in Sandspit. I knew our dollars in the bank would like more company.

"Need you to help Jim in Englefield Bay for three weeks. He can show you the ropes," said George Smith, of the Fisheries Department, after I accepted the charter and we had agreed on terms. "You'll be in Tasu for the last eight weeks of the season."

Two persons are required on each patrol boat. Gene would have been an ideal assistant, but he was in Viet Nam. "Our boat's too small for a third, nonfamily crew member to rub shoulders and tempers with for eleven weeks. And Betty's not about to stay ashore."

Husband and wife teams were a fairly new concept, but Mr. Smith agreed. "Just remember, the law requires you to pay your assistant at least nine-fifty a day."

"Okay," I laughed. "I'm a big spender. I'll give her ten."

After unloading our beachcombings and bones—it took two years of weathering before the jaws were fit to bring inside—we scrubbed down the boat and ourselves. A few clothes went through three washings; most went into the fireplace.

In Queen Charlotte City we topped off the fuel tanks and picked up a new crystal for the radio. We could now communicate with the office and all patrol boats and planes.

On a sunny August afternoon we caught the flood tide through Skidegate Narrows. Near Trounce Inlet we met *Sooke Post*. I tried out our radio, but we had to call out to each other as we passed. Whose radio had failed? That was the beginning of eleven weeks of communications frustrations.

There were no fishing boats at Kaisun Creek, on the north side of Englefield Bay, only the old V.T.G., skippered by Jim Carmichael, a thick-chested, happy-go-lucky Irishman, raised in the Charlottes, and an old acquaintance. Jim was rigging a mooring buoy near the creek mouth; he had dropped his anchor and the ancient winch refused to bring it back up.

Jim taught me how to tell the leaping, side-slapping chums from the splashing pinks. When the main run arrived—probably within a few days, for the patrol plane reported great schools just off the coast—we would have four streams to watch. Jim would guard the largest, Kaisun Creek. Betty and I would have a creek in MacKenzie Cove and two in Security Cove.

"Gotta watch those seiners," Jim warned one day as our boats gently rubbed sides and we sat in the sun enjoying mugs of coffee brewed by his assistant, Jim Monroe, a tall, laconic, blond-bearded young man from Queen Charlotte City.

In order to distinguish the two Jims when we were talking, we called them Captain Jim and Big Jim. "Can't call them Young Jim and Old Jim, because they're younger than either of us," I told Betty.

"Takes an old creek robber to really know how those fellows think," Captain Jim continued, a smile on his face. "They'll work in pairs. One lures the guardian away from the creek, out of sight. Then the other boat zips in and makes a fast set. Ten minutes or less, and they can clean out all the salmon waiting to go upstream. They can make a season's wages in one set. Can do it in the dark too."

Captain Jim shook his sandy-haired head and grinned like a young kid, perhaps recalling more exciting days. "Gotta watch 'em all the time. Every one of 'em!"

Canada geese nesting in the Charlottes were forming into flocks, feeding near the stream mouths, fattening up for their long flight. Late in the afternoon the V.T.G. often came into Security Cove and tied up alongside. Betty would serve a meal of delicious, freshly caught Dungeness crab, and we would all have an hour or so of gab. The flaming sunsets and smooth water made for pleasant evenings.

During one of these get-togethers, Captain Jim told of a seiner caught robbing a creek—an event I suspect did not happen frequently.

"The fog was thick and soggy. Skipper couldn't see the bow of his boat. Just the weather he'd been waitin' for. Had his compass courses and times all marked down. This was before all boats had one or two radars. Fish were jumping and splashing all around. Sounded like being under a waterfall, they were so thick. The creek robbers made their set and were pursing up when they heard a plane fly over. They laughed at any pilot crazy enough to fly in that weather! Had about two thousand salmon. All hands—even the cook—were brailing like mad when that float plane roars out of the fog and the fisheries officer yells, 'You're under arrest!' "

"How'd they find the boat in that fog?" Big Jim asked, shaking the dregs from his cup over the side.

"Was one of those thick, low fogs. The kind that hugs the water. Just high enough to cover the pilot house and leavin' the mast sticking up in the clear and surrounded on three sides by trees. Just one of those freak things that happens. And it couldn't have been at a worse time for the skipper and his crew." Captain Jim shook his head sadly.

"That pilot had lots of guts, too, landing blind on the water!" I said. "Might have hit a deadhead. He must have used the mast to give him an idea of height."

The salmon arrived. Their return to the stream of their origin is a remarkable achievement; their parents were dead before they were hatched, and eighteen months ago there were none of their kind to lead them to salt water. Yet they had returned from the vast feeding grounds of the North Pacific to their own stream.

On Sunday seventeen seine boats roared into Englefield Bay. Some trailed their skiffs; most packed them on the stern, lashed to the big net drum. At 6:00 p.m. fishing would begin.

By 5:30 p.m. every seiner had its skiff in the water, with two or three men on the fantail checking lines, testing hydraulic drives, smoking, talking, or slugging down a last coffee before the long hours of competitive fishing began. Half the skippers had located schools of pinks and were jealously tracking them, impatiently waiting for six o'clock to roll around. Two young skippers raced from bay to bay trying to decide where to fish. Three of the old timers leaned nonchalantly over their dodger, smoking and enjoying coffee as though they were on a vacation cruise.

Captain Jim was patrolling Kaisun Creek and Boomchain Bay. We were near MacKenzie Cove and in a position to keep an eye on the entrance to Security Inlet. There weren't many jumpers in that inlet.

Captain Jim announced the opening. He didn't have time to hang up his microphone before black diesel exhaust belched from racing engines and white water swirled under their counters. Skiffs were left astern of every seiner. Fathoms of dark net spun off the big drums as each skipper raced to encircle the largest number of fish in the least time—so he could begin the second and third sets. This was no sport; this was earning a living.

At times the rules of the nautical road were ignored or perhaps they were not fully understood. It was every boat for itself. One of the older and slower boats was almost on top of a school, executing a tight turn as its net rolled off the drum, when a new boat raced in, head on, turned inside, cast loose its skiff, made the set, and scooped the salmon out of the older boat's net.

I couldn't hear the words screamed above the pounding diesels as they passed within feet of each other, but I have heard similar outbursts with much less provocation. There was no danger that the captain of the older boat would cut across the other net; a propeller wrapped with seine net would put his boat out of the fishing for hours, or longer.

"Wonder what those two crews will do if they meet ashore," Betty mused before going below.

We stayed out of the way. These were fast sets. A quick circle, secure the outboard end amidships, purse up the bottom, and begin reeling in on the big drum or through the topped-up power block. There were no spectacular catches; five hundred or six hundred pinks was the best.

After the initial flurry, fishing slowed.

"Some of the boats are getting so few fish," I told Betty when she handed me a steaming cup of coffee, "that they don't bother with the brail. They just roll the net in over the stern and let the pocket of salmon spill on deck."

"Maybe it'll pick up next week. I hope so." Betty's grandfather had been a pioneer in the Puget Sound salmon industry, and she knew how much a good season meant to the families.

All the boats were catching the fisherman's plague: jellyfish. Thousands of them! Most were about the size of a soup bowl, though a few of the sea blubbers were nearly as large as a wash tub. The soft, oozy bodies flowed into the nets, becoming a gelatinous mass of stinging acid difficult to clean off and impossible to avoid, even if one was wearing forearm-length rubber gloves. The jellyfish ranged in color from milk-white through assorted shades of red, yellow, and purple. Under other circumstances, they might have been pretty.

Long after dark we anchored behind a slight point in MacKenzie Cove. The seiners were all heading for the rolling anchorage at Kaisun Creek or Boomchain Bay to unload into packers before grabbing a few hours of sleep.

Skylark began to roll as the tide flooded. It was near dawn. I began patrol. Seiners raced into view.

Before the middle of the flood tide schools of salmon swam into the cove, safe inside the "No commercial fishing" boundaries—large, white-painted triangles nailed conspicuously to trees on each side of a bay or inlet.

Here they would jump enthusiastically, perhaps in order to shake off sea lice (parasitic copepods). About the middle of the ebb tide they would flow back to sea, into the fishing area, their numbers decreasing with every change of tide. Each tide reduced the distance the salmon strayed from their stream.

The nightly tally of the salmon delivered to packers and reported via radio to the office in Queen Charlotte City confirmed that the fishing in the Charlottes was poor.

"The only sure thing about commercial fishing," Betty said, "is that it's a great gamble."

Closure was announced for 6:00 p.m. Wednesday. From then until 6:00 p.m. Sunday, salmon were free to come and go without human molestation. *Escapement* is the official term for this period.

Days of closure were days to hike the streams. Unless it was raining hard, these were enjoyable jaunts through lovely virgin country abounding with great stands of cedars, spruce, and hemlocks. Ivan, our Samoyed, would leap into the small boat whenever I slid into my waterproof caulked boots.

Ashore, I would shove a few cartridges into my .32 Special, and we were off. Ivan liked these outings, and since he wasn't trained for bears—I didn't have a clue how to teach him—I lugged the rifle as insurance. I didn't want to shoot, but if Ivan riled one and came running for help with an angry bear hot on his trail, I wanted to be the one who walked away.

Stream levels fluctuated according to the previous twelve to twenty-four hours of rainfall. These short streams were gradually filling. Salmon, and often trout, were in nearly every pool. Other salmon wriggled and splashed upstream through the shallows. I counted the three-to-six-pound pinks and the eight-to-twelve-pound chums. A few red-bellied coho spawned in one stream. The numbers of each species in each stream were reported during our evening radio conference.

Of the three streams Betty and I were watching, the one in Security Cove near an unused cabin was my favorite. Large meadows covering some two acres bordered the stream's wide, shallow mouth. Ramrod-straight spruce stood at parade-rest in open formation behind the lush meadow. Sphagnum moss and broad-leaved ferns carpeted the valley floor and blanketed fallen trees. Short grasses and scattered clumps of low salal grew in the open patches that got the sun. At dawn or dusk deer browsed here.

Over the years violent gales had slammed into the valley, knocking down massive trees. Some fell across the streams, driving their thick limbs deep into the gravel. Gushing water sluiced through these natural dam gates, and salmon fought this powerful flow as they responded to a primordial instinct to spawn. Tree trunks, old and limbless, lay in the stream, silt and fine gravel trapped on the upstream side. Smooth, rounded sheets of crystal-clear water rolled over the worn trunks, shaping small pools where salmon rested—sanctuaries from gulls, ravens, and eagles; hunting areas for hungry bears.

Deep pools below a sharp bend, scoured by spring and fall freshets, were the salmons' prime resting spots. A moving shadow might startle them. Their mottled sides would flash as they flitted upstream or down, propelled by tails and fins worn white and fleshless, even stripped and tattered until they looked like harlequins wearing an old shirt with slashed sleeves and torn tail. Their strength was ebbing. They had to spawn soon. Was there anything in their dim yet complex brains telling them they were also dying?

On one of my jaunts I saw a small female pink weighing perhaps three or four pounds, barely covered with water, lying in the gravel. Abruptly, with wide, violent thrusts of her tail, she began sweeping the gravel aside, her worn pectorals anchoring her above the chosen spot. A shallow excavation soon appeared as the current rolled the pebbles downstream. Swaying within inches of the female fish was a larger hump-backed, hook-jawed male, who attacked any other male approaching this territory.

Satisfied with her redd, the female dropped back a few inches until her deep belly fitted into the hollow and began expelling eggs—four or five thousand of them. Drifting aside, she made way for her mate, who quickly moved in and ejected his milt. Both brushed gravel over the fertilized eggs that would hatch in the spring, if they were not washed out by a destructive flood, covered with silt from an upstream landslide, uncovered by other spawning salmon, left dry by a diversion of the stream, nosed out and devoured by hungry Dolly Varden, or destroyed by some other act of capricious nature.

If the eggs did manage to hatch, the alevins would have to elude such predators as trout, mergansers, and seals. The odds were against them. Few would live to return to this stream.

Exhausted, their two-year life cycle completed, the pair of pink salmon drifted away.

Fishing did improve during the second week, and it was even better the third. Now we had to contend with increasingly violent winds and rough water. A seine skiff was flipped by a fitful gust. The fisherman was caught and hauled aboard the seiner—its best catch that day. Jellyfish were thicker than ever—something we had thought impossible. Rolling, angled decks were treacherously slippery with portions of these sea invertebrates. Nets were a slimy, stinging mess. The fishermen worked hard for every dollar they made.

Captain Ken Harley and the *Sooke Post* seemed to be everywhere. We would see him in the morning and then hear him on the radio calling from Kano Inlet, to the north, or from Tasu, to the south.

At the end of that third week we were ordered to go to Tasu Sound—whenever we deemed the seas suitable. Tasu is in another fishing area, and the season would open there soon. The sea calmed and we headed out. A pair of oars was flipped from our skiff as we bounced and plunged. After a particularly violent roll and crash into a breaking comber, I was wondering if I should have stayed at the missile center. The working conditions were certainly better there.

On Sunday a baker's dozen of seiners came into Tasu, followed by three little gillnetters. Two were high-speed aluminum boats manned by Cree Indians. Crees are fine fishermen. Many first came to British Columbia during the war to replace interned Japanese fishermen.

Tasu Sound is large and has five good salmon streams, plus a few lesser ones debouching into four bays and three inlets. The pinks and chums were schooling up in significant numbers in only two of these streams, so most of the seining and gillnetting was taking place in one bay. Otherwise slow *Skylark* could not have kept up.

All of nature was preparing for fall and winter; salmon were spawning, land birds and waterfowl were feeding, bears were patrolling the streams in search of salmon, and fat Sitka black-tailed bucks were polishing their antlers on the pliable alders and getting ready to go a'courting. Skies were often leaden, filled with chill rain and blustery winds. Fishing was poor.

When we were in Englefield Bay, Captain Jim checked the

daily catch and made the nightly report. Now these chores added two or three hours to my daily stint. Waiting until the last seiner or gillnetter unloaded into the packer's brine tanks, I could count on getting back to *Skylark* about 10:00 p.m.; then I made my report.

The time was no problem unless "Red" and some other character in Alaska were jabbering on their powerful radios. They used a U.S. frequency so close to the Canadian fisheries frequency that there was no getting on the air until they finished. So there were long days and short nights—and sometimes short tempers.

Reports of fish taken combined with my counts of salmon in the streams determined the duration of fishing each week. Although fishing always began on Sunday, closure might be as early as Tuesday evening.

Instead of waiting in Tasu during closure, some fishermen chartered flights to Prince Rupert or Vancouver. A few boats hurried to Queen Charlotte City for fuel and water and a few nights at the pub or Legion Hall for the crew.

One evening the packer failed to arrive. None of the boats were loaded, so there was no panic. A stiff southeaster had stirred up the sound all day, and some of the boats had not pulled away from the float. When a packer arrived the following day, we learned that our missing packer had taken shelter in Flamingo Inlet. During the night she dragged anchor and damaged both screws on the beach before limping back to Vancouver.

Disappointed with fishing in Tasu, seiners shoved off for what they optimistically hoped would be better fishing along the mainland coast. The gillnetters were doing fairly well, but they too departed for the mainland.

There were only six seiners in Tasu when the first big storm of fall struck. For two days it built up on the east coast. Abruptly, in the afternoon, just as the tide changed to flood and an eleven-foot run-in began, the winds cascaded down the mountains—a williwaw—attacking from every pass and valley with violent force. We were caught near the middle of the sound.

The modest, white-capped waves suddenly rose into high, charging crests. *Skylark* barely held steerageway. At times we ceased all forward movement and perhaps even went backward. Then there was a lull and we went ahead for a short distance. The townsite faded behind a drape of giant raindrops. The nearest land was a washed-out blob of gray.

"Think we can make it, or should we turn around and go into Two Mountain Bay?" Betty asked, salt water streaming down her face.

"*Skylark's* safe enough. We'll go into Tasu. Or backward into Two Mountain Bay."

Our antenna snapped like a buggy whip. The staff bearing the Canadian flag broke and, like a magic carpet, the flag flew horizontally through the rain, landing two hundred yards astern, a fleck of red and white on the heaving sea. Between waves, *Skylark* came about, and we quickly overtook the flag—our symbol of patrol duty—and snagged it with a pike pole. It took us over a half-hour to cover the last mile to Hunger Harbour, below the townsite.

For thirty-six hours we bounced, jerked, and rolled alongside the float. The seiners made no attempt to fish. Nature had scheduled her own salmon escapement, filling streams to overflowing, washing out, burying, and destroying many of the eggs already spawned. Nearly three inches of rain fell in forty-eight hours.

This was the last week of fishing. Our patrol lasted two more weeks, time to make final checks of the streams and to count the late spawners. The eggs of these late salmon might be the only ones to survive. Trained fisheries officers calculate the approximate number of spawning beds each stream provides. Beyond that number, late arrivals might uncover too many redds. Since all Pacific salmon die after spawning, fish arriving after the stream's capacity is reached are a total waste. Because the storm prevented fishing, hundreds, possibly thousands, of salmon went upstream instead of being caught.

The days after the storms were a time of feasting for bears, eagles, ravens, crows, gulls, and mergansers. Bright red eggs and white to purple salmon carcasses washed out onto gravel bars at all stream mouths.

Each rainstorm further purged the streams. Dolly Varden and trout fattened on loose, wasted eggs. Steelhead, fresh in from the ocean, arrived to gulp their share.

During hikes along the streams I often encountered bears. A shout, a whistle, or any loud noise let them know I was near, and they usually lumbered off into the forest. Bears hate to be interrupted; whatever they are doing is important to them, especially eating. They would move away, stop, and look over their shoulder, and, if I continued to move, so did they. Once I found a mature bear curled up asleep under the dry and hollowed-out roots of a large tree. I didn't wake it for its next meal—that might be me.

Only once did I have trouble scaring a bear. It was an old sow, probably so deaf and with such poor eyesight that she didn't know I was around. I was within twenty-five feet of her—across a shallow stream—before she heeded my yell. Grumbling and reluctant, she slowly moved away—but not out of sight.

Until a few years before, it had been the policy—either tacit or announced—to shoot bears near a spawning stream. Fishermen helped foist this senseless slaughter onto an uninformed or gullible public, just as they had pressed for the five-dollar bounty paid for each seal nose recovered and presented to the proper government office. I have read that for every seal nose recovered, another nine seals were killed and lost. Fortunately, the Fisheries Department came to realize that bears, seals, and sea lions are part of our great natural resources.

Many people have seen colorful paintings of a bear

standing in a white-water stream, paw upraised, ready to swat a salmon attempting to leap a rocky falls. Often a cub or two are on shore nipping into a flopping silver-sided salmon. This image is more picturesque than the more realistic image of a bear scavenging salmon cadavers cast on the banks of a stream that has recently overflowed.

During the third week of October, we received orders to return to Queen Charlotte City. Captain Harley offered to escort us with the *Sooke Post*, but we declined, deciding we were too slow for her.

Fall storms were now more frequent, lasted longer, and left the North Pacific angrier. It was too late to make our trip up Graham Island. "Another year," I promised Betty before she flew to Juneau, Alaska, to do more research on the wreck of the *Clarksdale Victory* and a couple of other vessels lost in the Charlottes. I left for Seattle to do my Naval Reserve training.

The bank account was replenished. In fact, it looked so good that we decided to take a three-month trip around the world by air and, if possible, to meet Gene in Singapore during his R & R from Viet Nam.

We did even better. We surprised him in Saigon and then met a few weeks later in Singapore. For thirty years I had wanted to see that exotic seaport.

"Ten days in Singapore," I told Betty as we lifted off for Kathmandu, Nepal, "was worth every moment of those long days and nights bouncing around on *Skylark*!"

10

Spring Cruise

Early one April we set out for a month's cruise along the west coast of Graham Island. With us was Peter Mylechreest, a handsome young doctor from the Lake District in England.

The doctor was one of our favorite crew members. Coming aboard with his black bag, he was recorded in *Skylark's* log as Ship's Surgeon. Peter enjoyed the title's nautical ring but never let it deter him from performing any of the many tasks required aboard a small boat.

Near midafternoon on our first day out, we rounded the last rocky point sheltering us from the open ocean. *Skylark* suddenly leaped and bucked. High, cresting combers swept across the wide mouth of Skidegate Channel, exploding against the bleak headlands of Chaatl Island.

Betty and Peter didn't offer any advice, but they were happy when I turned toward the protected waters of Dawson Inlet. Hidden behind a ragged point was a logger's abandoned float camp. It was old and the floats were awash, but it would be a safe moorage for the night.

During our sleep the waves spent their fury, and shortly after dawn we met smooth, easy rollers of only four to six feet.

Ahead, two points off the starboard bow, the low profile of Hunter Point jutted seaward. A reef stretched nearly a mile into the ocean, lava fangs waiting to tear into the underbelly of any unwary vessel.

Skylark leaped and twisted. Her small boats strained their lashings. Amidst a cacophony of loosened cups caroming about the cabin, we skirted the reef's turbulent waters. Beyond, the seas relented, and our boat rolled and pitched at regular intervals.

A half-mile distant to starboard, locked among towering boulders, lay a mass of twisted, rusted frames and plates—the skeletal remains of the *Kennecott*. A new U.S. ship, the *Kennecott* had run aground on Hunter Point at midnight on October 9, 1923, during a gale. Days earlier she had departed from Cordova, Alaska, with over six thousand tons of high-grade copper ore—a million-dollar cargo—headed for the smelter in Tacoma, Washington. Although the *Kennecott* and most of her cargo were lost, all hands were saved.

About fifty yards to the left of the remains of the *Kennecott* lay another wreck. Hunter Point's second major victim was one of the world's largest barges, costing over $1.5 million. It was being towed home to Portland, Oregon, almost empty, having discharged cargo consigned to the DEW Line. Miles off the Charlottes, the towing cable parted. Current, seas, and howling wind combined to carry the unmanned barge shoreward. The wild seas defeated all attempts to get a line aboard it from the tug, and breakers tossed the massive barge high ashore, almost on top of the *Kennecott*. Broken timbers, bashed fuel drums, and twisted axles mounting sets of dual wheels were all that remained to mark the disaster.

Near the head of Kano Inlet a small rain squall dispersed the sun's rays, forming a brilliant rainbow. I poked my head into the cabin. "Betty, we'll find the treasure for sure! A rainbow's marking the spot."

For the past six years Betty had been searching for information about five American vessels wrecked on the Charlottes' west coast. After anchoring in the shallow water of a boulder-rimmed pocket, we began looking for any sign of a small dock or loading platform. The doctor was in his Canova and ready to check along the shoreline. Betty and I would investigate the islands.

We found nothing on the first island and were about to land on the second one when Betty shouted, "Green barnacles!" By chance we had arrived near a cluster that was predominantly green instead of the usual dull ivory color, suggesting the presence of copper ore.

"We've found it!" Betty shouted, dropping to her knees and dipping her fingers into a soup-bowl-sized niche to retrieve a brilliant chunk of malachite, which had lain there for nearly half a century. She hefted it. "Nothing but rich ore is that heavy."

Spying our activity, Peter planed along the mirrored water until he almost reached the island; then he cut the motor and leaped ashore ahead of the wake, painter in one hand, camera in the other.

Casting about like kids on a treasure hunt, we continued to locate scattered spills, filling our pockets with heavy ore. Betty uncovered part of a hessian ore sack that was interwoven with moss but still strong.

While Betty prepared supper, Peter cleaned and polished abalone shells discarded by feeding otters. He sat on a stubby, beachcombed soya sauce keg, using one of his dental tools as a scraper. Although he was an M.D., he sometimes did emergency dental work.

"What's the other thing you and Betty want to find?"

"A raft. We think it's part of a trans-Pacific raft—the violent end of someone's dream.

"After World War II it became a fad to cross the Pacific on a raft. I don't know how many tried it. Some alone. Most with two or three persons, including, occasionally, a woman. It reached its peak by the midfifties. Financed by private funds or supported by public subscription, rafts costing thousands of dollars were launched. Some sailed in the name of science. Some for adventure. Others just wanted to get away from the confusion of postwar civilization and do something on their own. Some were rescued only miles off the California coast. Others disappeared. A few succeeded. Whatever the end, raft stories were always big news on the West Coast.

"It was late in the evening two summers ago when we found the raft. The sea was in a rare mood—flat calm. Since dawn, Betty and I had been beachcombing, making easy landings on heretofore unapproachable beaches, loading *Skylark* with glass balls, bamboo, plastic floats, Japanese kegs, and saki bottles.

"We were headed for Port Louis and a night's rest. Naturally we were scanning the shore. The wreckage lay fifty feet above the water. I figured it was a plane.

"Ashore we discovered it to be part of a raft, tossed high by a tsunami, probably one created by the Chilean earthquake of 1961, or the quake in Anchorage in 1964. We took measurements and a few pictures. It was too late for a thorough search, but the raft appeared to be homemade, of heavy-gauge galvanized sheet metal, decked with three-quarter-inch marine plywood and fastened with rusted bolts and screws.

"In the emergency equipment locker I found a rusted hatchet—its wooden handle disintegrated in my fingers; a rusted yet watertight box full of distress flares; and an unused log book with a sharpened pencil. There was a small distilling unit too."

"Don't forget the little boat compass," Betty interjected. "That was in its own small box and wrapped with torn paper from a Portland, Oregon, newspaper."

"Not a clue as to who made it or where they launched," I

continued, "or if the sailors were fortunate enough to survive."

"Let's eat," Betty said. We were ready. The small cabin was filled with the aroma of good food.

"The raft's on a nasty piece of coast," I said sitting down, "and we haven't been able to make another landing."

We talked and planned until late. Tired and content, full of thick venison steaks, we fell asleep, lulled by the boat's gentle roll.

The days were full. We plodded northward, walking remote beaches, picking up glass balls and any other drift of interest. "Betty, this will go on the ladder to our sleeping loft." I held up a shaped oak handrail from a wrecked boat. "That's the first thing I've found this trip that I knew exactly where we could use it."

We landed through low surf on Hippa Island, sparkling under a bright spring sun, and began the two-mile hike to another shipwreck. We walked up steep hills, over hummocks, down defiles, and through windrows of tangled, storm-felled trees whose upturned limbs stretched out to snare our clothes as we passed. For deer or bear, it was a trail; for us, an obstacle course.

On the southwest side of the island our path led across sharp black basalt and around long fingers of frothing sea crashing through clefts in ancient lava flows. We passed tall columns of weathered magma, a few topped with one or two straggly trees.

The tide was out. We hiked across the rough reef to the broken wreck. The huge bow loomed high above our heads, an insurmountable, rusty cliff. Thick wires that once hoisted and lowered cargo to and from the holds dangled with whiskered ends from rusted blocks. Heavy anchor chain draped across the bow indicated a futile attempt to save the ship—and survive. Large letters, just discernible, high on the port bow spelled out the name: U.S.A.T.S. *Clarksdale Victory.*

"Home for Thanksgiving!" was the happy greeting

between shipmates as this U.S. Army ship steamed away from the dock in Whittier, Alaska, in 1947. "Next stop, Seattle."

Bad weather, the vagaries of ocean currents, and a sudden fall gale combined to set the ship some twenty-five miles east until her course lay across Hippa Island's raging reef. In the on-again, off-again visibility of a stormy evening the vessel struck the reef and stranded at high tide. Throughout a seemingly endless night, wild seas washed aboard the powerless, blacked-out ship, battering men and steel. A cold, wet, hazy dawn revealed that the ship was broken; only the bow section remained.

Ashore, where raging seas had cast them, five injured, chilled, oil-drenched seafarers huddled in tattered clothing. Four lived to be the only survivors of a crew numbering fifty-three men. "A genuine old-fashioned shipwreck in this modern age," I said to Peter as we stared at the broken hulk.

A fur seal sunned beside a quiet pool near the wreck. She was old. Unable to keep pace with the migrating herd, she had chosen this solitary spot to die. She bared her broken yellow teeth as we approached with our cameras.

After finishing our sandwiches and searching the beach, we headed back to *Skylark* and on toward Athlow Bay. The next day, we spotted the raft resting above the sea. After battling stormy seas, we found a quiet cove and went ashore to do some beachcombing.

A winter storm had toppled a large spruce. Its shallow roots stood on edge; they were over twelve feet high. From habit I moved into the circle of uncovered soil and rocks. For about 150 years the tree had hidden these rocks, which were blackened and cracked by campfires. Amidst the grays and blacks lay a light-green stone. I felt its smooth surface. Turning it over, I gazed into a small carved face. Carefully I scraped and cleaned my fist-sized artifact. It was a piece of a stone bowl.

Betty and Peter came running in response to my excited yell. We searched for the remainder of the bowl without success. No chart or map showed this area to be part of an ancient village, but some Natives had been here.

"Let's scout around," Betty said eagerly. "Who knows what more we might discover?"

Scattering, we walked through the open forest, where a springy carpet of green and gold sphagnum moss silenced our movements. Fallen trees were the only hindrances until I came to a high, overhanging cliff, its flat gray face masked by a beard of bright orange lichens. The cliff looked away from the sun; yet this treeless ledge was dry. Any dry spot in the Charlottes' rain forests is rare. "A good campsite," I said to myself.

Then I noticed the Haidas had decided on another use. Two boxes of wide, split cedar boards, grooved and then folded into a square, had been secreted here. They were burial boxes; the Haidas folded the bodies of their dead and returned them to the prenatal position before fitting them into the boxes. Bleached bones were scattered about the colorful, sheltered ledge.

The following morning we again turned northward. Peter, a biologist by avocation, was first to sight the congery of eagles. "There's at least fifteen and maybe eighteen," Peter said, lowering the binoculars. "I've never seen so many eagles at one time!"

Some perched in twisted, broken trees. A few sat on the shore, gorged and reluctant to fly. Recent arrivals slashed with curved beaks at a dark mass lying above the receding tide.

"Probably an overripe bull sea lion," I said. "But let's go ashore and see."

We had stopped and were drifting in an open roadstead aptly named Peril Bay. Frederick Island and its contiguous half-submerged reef and kelp bed offered quiet shelter. Peter dropped the anchor. Its rattling chain scared the feeding eagles. With wings spanning over six feet and flapping slowly, they rose to fly off a short distance, screaming at us with high, sharp notes. Circling above or settling on a tree, they watched, hoping we would soon depart.

The slim mammal was some type of a beaked whale unlike any we had seen before. Its skin was smooth and glossy black; its dorsal fin, small and placed far back. A single, flat, triangular tooth grew from each side at the midsection of the lower jaw; these teeth were exposed outside the closed mouth.

Betty went back to the boat to get our whale identification book. With the aid of the book's drawings and descriptions, we made the identification. "It's a rare Stejneger's beaked whale!" Betty exclaimed. "A male. And the book says they've had only four specimens to study."

We have been married long enough that I knew what she was going to say next.

"We've got to save this for the Provincial Museum."

"Uh-huh." I was doing my best to sound enthusiastic. I must have overacted because I found myself making a radio telephone call to the curator of the museum in Victoria.

"Yes! Yes! Of course we want the complete skeleton! No we can't possibly get to Frederick Island. You're there. Just bring it to Sandspit and ship it air express. A little meat on the bones won't hurt anything! Kind of you to call. Good-bye for now."

The whale looked a lot bigger than its sixteen feet. It had recently washed ashore and was far from being a skeleton. We couldn't even turn it over.

"Those scientists are going to have to be content with just a fleshy head," I declared after tying a line around the tail and securing it to a tree. "If they want any more, they can find it here."

I expected help, at least professional advice, from the Ship's Surgeon. Without a moment's hesitation, Peter declined. "I've done my share of autopsies. I'm going beachcombing—after I grab a few shots of you playing Jack the Ripper."

Betty was already up to her elbows.

We began work, and the carefree beachcomber soon departed. I began slashing, my six-inch sheath knife substituting for a flensing knife. The thin, dark skin and gray, oleaginous blubber were soft; the ligaments, tough and cordlike. At last, while glaucous-winged gulls wheeled and swooped overhead, shrieking loudly, I severed the head from its articulating vertebra. Peter returned in time to help carry the skull to the boat—after we had tightly wrapped it in layers of heavy plastic.

That old bogey, time, was closing in on us. The calendar showed that we had been out nearly three weeks, but it seemed more like a long weekend.

High northwest swells rhythmically lifted *Skylark* on rounded crests and gently lowered her into glassy troughs, carrying us homeward at a fast, pleasant pace.

Arriving off the southern shore of Hunter Point, we found this, the lee side, to be quiet enough for an easy landing. The tide was beginning to flood, so *Skylark* would be raised safely above any unseen rocks.

High on a jackstraw pile of drift logs lay a rusted Japanese mine. "It's safe. The explosive's dissolved out," I pointed to the hole in the case. "These drifting mines were an ever-present danger to all ships sailing north of the equator during the war. I shot and sank a couple of them." I twisted off two of the brass, chemically activated horns as souvenirs. Although they were bashed and bent, the characters could still be read.

A breeze wafted through Skidegate Channel. Dazzling cumulus clouds drifted across a deep blue sky. The sun sparkled, silvering the rippled sea and warming us as we stood on deck, relaxed and happy, admiring our enchanting surroundings. Steep, verdant hills bounded the channel on either side; seabirds dove for little fishes.

Steam rose from our cups as we relived our adventures and toted up our beachcombed harvest. Peter's collection included three large glass balls, one covered with net; a rare rolling-pin-shaped glass float; nearly three dozen small glass balls; assorted seashells; and rolls of exposed color film—everything he had wanted and more.

Betty was happy with her small but heavy sack of copper ore from the wrecked *Kennecott*, plus many balls, bottles, and lengths of bamboo.

I prized the little stone face and a brightly painted life ring from the *Daian Maru* out of Akashi, Japan. I hoped the museum staff would be happy with their package containing the whale skull. (Two years later we found the remains of a female Stejneger's beaked whale and sent that skull to the Provincial Museum.) Another time we would try to reach the mystery raft.

11

Fighting Cohos

Our friends George and Sherry, along with three of their friends from Texas, came up to do some salmon fishing one weekend in late September.

"Where's the salmon?" George demanded as soon as he stepped off the plane. With three rod cases and a big green tackle box in his hands, he charged into the terminal at close to a run.

"Lots of cohos at Copper Bay and off the mouth of the Deena," I replied, laughing at his eagerness. "Think we'll do best at the Deena. It's been dry all summer. The big ones are just waiting for rain and a chance to go upstream."

"Could we start today?" George sounded hopeful.

"Of course! Everything's arranged—hotel, boats, and another pickup. Just shift into your fishing clothes, unless you're all so eager you want to go in those outfits." I glanced at George's two male companions, also in expensive business suits, and the two fashionably dressed women.

"I'd go right now," George stated, "but Sherry would wring my neck."

George had been a brilliant supply officer aboard a destroyer tender during the war. He was one of those remarkable men who studied the Bureau of Supply and Accounts Manual to find a way to do something, instead of searching for an obscure regulation to prevent issuing an item or paying a sailor. After the war he had entered the investment and insurance business, succeeding beyond his wildest dreams. Now, over twenty years later, he was beginning to take a few days off, playing as hard and seriously as he worked.

The fishing party hurried down the hotel steps, transformed from city folk into fishermen. George and Sherry sported matching flame-red windbreakers and rain hats. John and his handsome wife, Lupe, appeared in buttercup-yellow rain gear. Lupe's brown hair peeked from under a wide-brimmed safari hat bespangled with wet and dry flies and two "Big Fish" awards. Jack's sky-blue jacket matched the trim of his clan tartan cap.

"You all look great!" I said in unabashed admiration. "I hope the fish appreciate those Nieman-Marcus outfits."

We piled into the two pickups and headed for the Deena River. The first ten miles were over a good asphalt road clinging to the easy contours of Skidegate Inlet. We saw silvery cohos leaping near the bouldered shore as they swam toward one of the many spawning streams emptying into the inlet. From Alliford Bay to the Deena we drove on a private logging road of hard-packed gravel. A few miles beyond the log dump and sorting grounds at South Bay, we turned onto a short, rutted trail and down a steep embankment to a small beach.

In moments we unloaded the boats, mounted the outboards, loaded our tackle, and were underway for the river. George and Sherry were with me. On each rising tide the cohos eagerly entered the river mouth. Fall rains were abnormally late and there was not enough water for them to go upstream, so they drifted seaward with each ebb. Sighting dozens of leaping and cavorting salmon, we stopped in their midst.

"I've never seen so many salmon jumping. And such big ones!" Sherry exclaimed as George snapped a canoe spoon onto her line. I had seen bays filled with leaping salmon before, but it will always be a rousing sight.

"Hope you catch the first one, Sherry," said George as he cast. "I just want the largest!"

I didn't fish. Three of us casting from a twelve-foot boat would slow the action, and I could come here anytime. Soon it was apparent that the salmon were less than eager; we made more than four dozen casts without a strike. And twice we dropped lures almost on a coho's nose!

"Okay Neil," George said with a slight tone of impatience, "what's the secret lure catching them around here?"

I had been wondering the same thing. "Let's try an alligator on Sherry's line and that old standby, a crocodile, on yours." The dressed Mepps Aglia had failed me for the first time.

While George changed lures, I yanked the outboard into life. "We'll try closer to shore." A small flock of harlequin ducks and scoters scurried away as we neared a wall of black boulders rising straight from the bay before sloping back into a hairline of salal and stunted cedars high above the tide line. Gray lichens splotched the weathered rocks. Bright green moss clung tenaciously to thin, jagged cracks. An eagle eyed us warily from the topmost spire of a silvery snag.

"I think I hooked bottom," Sherry said quietly, slowly reeling in after her second cast. "But it feels free now."

"Reel in! Fast!" I said. "Might be a salmon. It's deep here."

Almost immediately a coho leaped in a wide arc, clearing the water by nearly two feet. Sherry's line jerked taut. Striking from behind, the coho had continued swimming toward the boat.

"Keep that tip up!" George reminded her, hastily retrieving his lure. "That's a fine-looking fish!"

Thin line arced across the bow as the salmon charged off in a powerful lunge. The large diamond on Sherry's left hand flashed as she spun the reel. The salmon jerked line out as fast as she reeled it in. Leaping, twisting, even charging, that coho fought desperately for over ten minutes before Sherry forced the tiring fish near the boat—only to see it suddenly become revitalized. The rod bent. The reel hummed, and line streaked through the teflon-lined guides as that darting coho tried frantically to rid itself of the hook. Gamely it fought, swimming in decreasing arcs until it was worn out. Sherry brought it alongside, where, with a weak flick of its tail, it rolled onto its side.

"That's a twelve-pound beauty!" I said, hefting the dripping prize.

"You fought that fish just right, Sherry," George said proudly. "He stood a better chance of getting off than you did of landing him."

Sherry just gazed at her salmon and smiled happily.

"Can't catch anything but ourselves," George said as he cast, "if we keep these lures in the boat."

A light southeast breeze played across the dull green bay, rippling the surface, stirring an occasional cat's paw. Farther offshore scattered whitecaps decorated the channel. A wisp of cloud hung over a tall mountain peak like smoke rising from a volcano.

Suddenly it was chilly. Unnoticed, the sun had slid behind the bald mountain peaks. Sherry quickly forgot the cold as another coho hit her lure. No doubt about this strike! In seconds fifty yards of monofilament was ripped off her spinning reel; then the salmon leaped out and did a tail-wiggling dance.

"That's bigger than your first one!" George yelled, while Sherry and the coho played their deadly game of tug-of-war. Soon she brought the fish alongside. I started to sneak the net under its head. Instantly, with a violent sideways snap, it dashed away. Two minutes later Sherry brought the beauty back, and we boated it.

This was a larger salmon, about the same length as the first but of greater girth, and it showed a tinge of pink on the belly.

Soon George had a few moments of sport with a grilse and then swung it aboard. "Just right for frying over the campfire."

"Right. Tomorrow I'll bring a pan and the Coleman stove. A coffee pot too," I promised.

It was getting late—time to head home. The other half of our party was already ashore and packing up. Jack was toting a nice pair of salmon— a ten-pounder he had landed and a shiny twelve-pounder Lupe had brought in. John had lost a salmon when his line tangled with the outboard.

"Not bad for a couple of hours' fishing," Lupe announced with a pleased smile.

Our drive home through the dark, tree-lined hills took close to an hour. We relived the afternoon, and John's lost fish gained weight as we speculated on its size.

"Look at that deer!" Sherry shrilled, as we rounded a sharp curve and the headlights picked up a fat buck with a nice set of polished antlers. The big Sitka black-tailed buck ran gracefully along the road, his fat belly swaying from side to side like a hammock.

"He's about as large as we see here," I said as the buck found a game trail and disappeared into the brush. "No big two-hundred-and-fifty-or-three-hundred-pound deer around here. Only one-hundred-to-a-hundred-and-fifty-pounders. Just right for eating and easy to pack out of the bush."

Sunday morning broke as one of those golden, crisp fall days called Indian Summer. There was no wind. By mid-morning it would be shirt-sleeve weather. Scenes along the inlet and streams were more beautiful than any calendar reproductions. A few incandescent cumulus clouds floated across the sky, along with a gaggle of Canada geese. The tide was low, changing to flood as we dragged the two metal boats across the gravel shore.

"We'll get our limit today," George announced confidently as he stepped into the boat.

For over an hour we made work of this recreation, without so much as a strike. Cast out and reel in; then cast again. The rhythm was interrupted only when we changed lures, trying different shapes, sizes, colors.

I poured three hot, black coffees from the thermos, and we tried to come up with a better strategy. Salmon were all around us, leaping from, or gliding through, the clear water. We had just not interested—or angered—them.

"Let's check with Jack," George suggested, "and see how they're doing."

A grilse for the frying pan and a possible strike were all Jack had to brag about.

"Let's do a little bucktailing," I suggested. "We sure aren't having any luck with metal lures." From my shirt pocket I pulled two small, silver-wrapped flies covered with polar bear hair and green filament hiding a single hook. We rigged a one-ounce weight twenty inches in front. We were the only people trolling.

"Strike!" George yelled on our second pass across the shallow bay. His rod was bent by a pugnacious coho. Sherry quickly brought in her line, and I tipped up the outboard. That fighter slammed back and forth at the end of the eight-pound test line for a few moments before clearing the rippled surface for a long, side-slapping leap.

"This fly must be what they want today," said George as he held up his silver prize. "Think he'll go twelve pounds?"

"Won't argue that till we check him on Jack's scales."

Sherry had a solid strike on our next run across the gravel flats, where clumps of underwater grass offered feed for the assorted ducks squawking and flying around. She was working the fish nicely. Suddenly, a slack line. It had broken.

"Tough luck," I said. "And worse, we don't have any more bucktails."

A half-hour before lunch George landed another coho. He was not a spectacular fighter, but he weighed in at 14½ pounds. Sherry caught a grilse on a tee spoon.

The six of us compared stories and scores as we lit a fire of dry cedar bark and beachwood on the pebbled shore. While the coffee perked atop the gas stove, Sherry and Lupe spread a fantastic array of foods ransacked from George's plane: Danish ham and cheeses, Russian caviar, pickled baby ears of corn, Mexican hot peppers, and, something I was more familiar with, a big jar of peanut butter. A large, weathered drift log served as our buffet table. Jack's boat had not struck any salmon since we had seen them at midmorning.

"A couple more hours to high tide," I said, glancing at my watch as we cleaned up the area and doused the fire. "Should be good fishing about now—if my Swedish neighbor's advice is any good."

We trolled across the shoal water. Nearing a narrow peninsula, I turned the boat in a wide, sweeping arc, crossing a patch of deep water. The bucktail must have been nearly motionless. Without warning, the line was ripped from George's reel; the rod bent. George stood up, feet wide apart, knees slightly bent—a real sailor's stance—as he fought that coho. This strong, determined fighter stayed deep, performing his escape tactics unseen. For over ten minutes George played that salmon, as line slowly came in and then rushed out in an exciting life-and-death struggle. The runs became shorter. After a pause to rest, the salmon struck out against the drag of reel and line.

"Feels like a big one!" George exclaimed. "He's tiring. And so am I."

At last the magnificent salmon quivered on the deck, and George dropped onto the seat. "That was some fight! Didn't know which of us would wear out first."

Slipping my fingers under the gill covers, I lifted the broad, copper-bellied fish. "Bet this one's close to twenty pounds."

The tide was almost high when we entered the river mouth. Salmon and fishermen were all around us. The river was too congested for trolling, so we resumed crisscrossing the flooded tidal flats.

George landed his fourth coho—the daily limit—a half-hour before dusk. "I'll put the bucktail on Sherry's line, and we'll give her a couple more passes before we quit."

Sherry soon hooked into a spirited fighter. Not a big fish, but a bright eleven-pounder.

"That's a new one on me," I said, heading for the pickups. "Never saw a day when cohos would strike only flies and refuse all types of metal lures."

"Believe me, we'll have a stock of bucktails when we come up next time," George said.

We were nearly unloaded when Jack zoomed in for a landing. Lupe displayed a bright coho weighing 15¼ pounds. John and Jack had been skunked.

"Hey, Jack," George called with a wide, boyish grin, "will you weigh my fish? Just the big one."

"No need to rub it in," Jack said, pulling out his pocket scales. The pointer slid past eighteen pounds and steadied opposite the twelve-ounce mark. "That's what I call a nice coho! Congratulations, George."

We loaded the boats into the pickups. We wouldn't be using them anymore this trip. Tomorrow we'd try river fishing on Graham Island.

Sometime during the night fog rolled in from Hecate Strait, wrapping us in a monochrome cocoon as we drove to Alliford Bay and then boarded the ferry for the twenty-minute ride across Skidegate Inlet.

The sun slowly burned off the fog on Graham Island.

Hecate Strait appeared beside us, calm and gray. The coastline was piled high with weathered drift logs, tossed like jackstraws far above the spring tide line—even into the trees—evidence of the violence of winter storms. Cormorants perched on off-lying rocks, and seagulls squatted on the sand.

Gravel-bottomed Tlell river is a tidal stream snaking through miles of low, flat land, often parallel with the coast, until it debouches across a shifting bar of gravel into Hecate Strait. At the river's bends are deep pools where salmon and trout rest, and hopeful fishermen test their skills. We parked near one of these crescent-shaped pools and began casting.

"I've got one!" Lupe cried. A real fighter, but his opportunities to show off were limited by the size of the pool. Lupe soon worked the fish into shallow water, and John slid a net under the hook-nosed buck coho. Redder than any we had taken in salt water, it weighed in at a trifle over fifteen pounds.

Lupe enjoyed fishing and swore by one lure, a small red and white dardevle. We teased her about using only one lure, but she must have known what she was doing—in less than ten minutes she had landed a lively grilse, while we were flogging the stream.

By lunchtime we had two Dolly Varden to go with Lupe's grilse in the frying pan and five cohos for the freezer.

When we returned to the pool it was nearly black and still—high tide. A gray, chill fog crept in from the straits, swirling below the treetops. There was no sign of fish. No leaping or finning. We fished on faith.

Again it was Lupe and her dardevle. What a salmon! He leaped, twisted, ran upstream and down, and then shot across to the undercut bank while Lupe struggled to keep her line taut. Her years of experience were needed for this one. If that fish could have found any submerged branch or root to entangle that thin line, he would have had it made. John stood by with the net and soon proudly carried it up the bank and laid it out on the grass for us to admire—and envy.

"Hey, George," John shouted. "We've got a twenty-pounder here. How about paying us that five bucks now?"

George slowly reeled in before answering. "Still another hour or so to fish." He eyed the fat salmon. "And you haven't weighed it yet."

Jack took time out to weigh Lupe's coho. "Eighteen-twelve," he sang out. "Exactly the same as George's big one of yesterday."

"It's a draw," George laughed. "We both win and have a nice catch to brag about too."

In that last hour four more salmon were landed. We had all done well, except unlucky John, who finished the trip without catching a thing. He was a good sportsman, however, and he was happy to see the pleasure Lupe derived from bringing home the family salmon.

Reluctantly we reeled in, broke down the rods, and stowed tackle boxes and salmon in the trucks.

That evening five happy fishermen and four boxes of choice salmon flew from the Charlottes, leaving behind promises to return next year.

12

Prospectors and Whalers

It was late fall and we were in Sandspit when Vince Edwards, pilot and coordinator for a mineral exploration crew, phoned to ask if the crew might base its camp in Puffin Cove the following summer. "It's the only adequate clearing for our campsite anywhere near the middle of the area to be prospected," Vince explained, "and we'd be there only six weeks."

We agreed, although we were reluctant to lose our privacy and have the serenity of Puffin Cove disturbed.

That was also the summer that Gene returned safely from Viet Nam. With him was his wife, Patty. They relinquished the cabin we had built for them or other guests and set up a tent across the lagoon.

The small cabin became the office and plotting room for Texas Gulf Sulfur's crew. Tents, propane stove and refrigerator, fuel, lumber, food, an inflatable boat with outboard, and all other items required to support six college-student pros-

127

pectors, a geologist, a cook, a pilot, and a helicopter engineer were flown in.

Under Vince's direction, four tents were quickly erected, plywood floors laid, stoves installed, and camp routine established. Vince and Don, the engineer, claimed the grassy glade under our tree-house tree.

They worked six days a week, weather permitting. Mornings were noisy, as the exuberant young men dashed about assembling their gear. Then there was the roar of the Bell helicopter being warmed up and building to full power for its check, followed by the distinctive thump-thump of its long rotor blades biting the air as Vince lifted off with two of the prospectors, taking them to some mountaintop for drop-off. Then the back-and-forth shuttle until three two-man teams, and sometimes the geologist, were in the field.

As the prospectors worked their way down the mountain-sides, usually alongside a stream or landslide, they bagged and tagged samples of silt to be flown to Vancouver for chemical analysis.

Sometimes Vince waited on the beach for a crew to come out of the bush to be picked up. More often he returned to camp so that Don could perform routine preventive maintenance on the helo. At least once a week he would fly into Sandspit to ship out samples, returning with mail and supplies. Sometimes, if he had space, he would invite Betty to go along. She never refused.

Even after a strenuous day on the mountainsides, the prospectors had energy to burn. For recreation they indulged in Frisbee contests, jumping rope, and running. Moving rocks and boulders to clear a path for the inflatable boat, fitting rocks into steps near the campsite, and building up a level spot above the high-tide line for the float-mounted helicopter were jobs made to look like fun.

Occasionally Vince took Betty and me from the warm lagoon to snowy mountaintops, landing on the crusted snow.

Or we might fly along the shore, landing to beachcomb a spot inaccessible by boat. Then we would lift off to sweep across a lily-fringed mountain lake we had seen only on charts. Sometimes Vince would take us through winding valleys crowded with lush timber and drained by purling salmon streams, their sides rising abruptly to grass- and flower-covered meadows where deer browsed or lay peacefully chewing their cuds and bears might be seen clawing out roots.

It was always a thrill to fly along steep cliffs, seeing uplifted, intruded, displaced, and angular rock faces, or to dash toward a sheer mountainside and abruptly stop, hovering fifty feet or so from these fascinating formations, and then slowly cross the grass-filled bowl of an extinct volcano. Best of all I enjoyed lifting over a hogbacked ridge to see a magnificent panorama of forested valleys and tiny lakes with the sea beyond—and then suddenly drop at fifteen hundred feet per minute as Vince threw out the clutch and let the helo autorotate, engaging the clutch a few hundred feet above ground level before zooming away in lazy arcs as we gazed at everything above, below, beside, and ahead of us. My stomach usually caught up with me before we landed at Puffin Cove.

For us, riding in a helicopter was addictive. I had ridden in them before, but never under such fun conditions.

On other days I might help Vince and Don bring in supplies, primarily fuel. Planes can't land at Puffin Cove, so an amphibious Goose or Beaver loaded with drummed fuel and boxes of food from Sandspit would land at an unnamed mountain lake—identified on forestry maps as Lake 242, its height in feet above sea level—on Moresby's east coast and discharge cargo on the shore.

We would hop over a sixteen-hundred-foot pass and load the gas and food into net slings. While Vince hovered four or five feet overhead, we would hook on the slings and wave him off, and away he'd go. In two or three fast trips everything was deposited in front of the camp.

Afternoons were also noisy as the helicopter came and went, bringing back muddy, sometimes drenched, always hungry crews. After hanging bags of samples in the sauna to dry and reporting their findings to the geologist, the crews were free to head for the sauna.

Don always fired it up before noon so the building was hot and the tank of water steaming. A sauna and hot tub were luxuries everyone appreciated.

"Our usual summer bathing," Vince told us, "is limited to a fast dip in some frigid, mosquito- and blackfly-infested lake or stream. This is civilization!"

The sauna required wood—lots of wood. About once a week some of the crew hiked to the outer beach with a chain saw. They would level a spot for the helo to land, and in an hour or so they would cut drift logs into a few sling loads of firewood. One weekend they surprised us by flying in two sling loads of stove wood, dropping it on the beach below the cabin. After shutting down the helo, Vince lined everyone up like a bucket brigade, and in five minutes we had enough wood to last us a month, piled beside the cabin. We never had it so good!

On a couple of evenings the crew gathered in our cabin for cocoa, tea, or coffee to go with the delicious warm cookies or cake that Phil, their outstanding cook, had prepared for the occasion. While we crowded on chairs, couch, bed, and floor, Vince enthralled us with tales of duty in exotic Malaysia, Hong Kong, and the Persian Gulf when he was an army pilot.

Our secluded hideaway now had a population of fourteen. By coincidence, that was the summer for the census. So one afternoon Vince brought in the pretty enumerator from Tasu to count heads and have dinner with the men. Some of the fellows were so unnerved at the sight of a woman in the mess tent that they were tongue-tied.

One day Betty, Patty, Gene, and I were beachcombing a few miles south of Puffin Cove when we heard the helo approaching. "I didn't think they were prospecting down this way," Gene said, as we watched the bird grow larger. Then Vince tipped and pointed to a rock in the bay, where he landed, balancing on one float. I rushed over in the skiff and opened the door on the passenger side. Vince nodded toward the seat. Both his hands and feet were occupied with flying. There was a box for us. With a shouted "thanks," I shut the door and crouched on the rock as he lifted off. I almost lost my hat in the rotor wash. After circling *Skylark*, Vince headed toward Puffin Cove.

Patty opened the box. "Sandwiches, cookies, and mail!" she shouted. "They're too good to us."

In July, Betty rode into Sandspit with Vince to be on hand when our five-year-old grandson, George II, arrived from California. While she was in the airport coffee shop, she heard about a committee that was busy preparing for a short visit by Queen Elizabeth and Prince Philip.

The committee had a problem—a big problem. A forty-foot gray whale had washed ashore near the end of the runway, within smelling distance of the site where the royal party was to be greeted. Prevailing winds were already wafting the rank odor to the air terminal.

In this area, where roads are being punched through, stumps removed, and mining performed, explosives are commonly used to expedite work. Dynamiting was suggested as the fastest way to get rid of the ripening whale. The idea was favorably received until someone mentioned that certainly the whale would be destroyed but that pieces would be scattered all over the runway and people to pick up the pieces would be scarce.

Betty was trying to figure out how she could get possession of the massive animal and skeletonize it—a task impossible to accomplish in the short time before the Queen arrived. The committee knew Caterpillars were available in the bush. But were there enough of them to push, pull, or roll the thirty-ton carcass away, or into a massive excavation?

Overnight, while the committee members pondered and worried, a high tide floated the whale away, depositing it on a beach two miles to the south. The committee literally drew a fresh breath.

Betty was also happy. No one wanted the whale, it wouldn't be destroyed, and it was now accessible by road. "My own whale to skeletonize!" she said jubilantly, hurrying away to get a length of line. With one end of the line tied around its tail and the other around a sturdy spruce, the whale wouldn't float away again. Then she put up a sign requesting that the bones not be removed. Probably there weren't too many people who would take them, but Betty was taking no chances.

Skeletonizing began—slowly and crudely. We had spent days at the whaling station at Coal Harbor on Vancouver Island watching forty- to ninety-foot giants being cut up, ready for total reduction in a half-hour. Betty didn't have flensing knives, massive toggles, wire cables, or steam winches to facilitate her work. She began with a sheath knife, a keyhole saw, and a lot of determination.

A few days later Vince flew into Puffin Cove with Betty and George II. Excitedly, Betty told me about this once-in-a-lifetime chance to skeletonize a gray whale. "Progress is slow. A few more weeks of warm sun will make our work easier," she said with assurance, conning me into a job that was to make work on the Stejneger's beaked whale look like good clean fun.

The community of Sandspit welcomed the Queen and her Consort, entertained them with Haida dancing, and presented them with a superbly carved argillite totem—all without offending the royal olfactory senses.

The longer the prospectors stayed, the more we hated to think of their leaving. Their kindness and unexpected services were spoiling us. We even tried to talk them into spending the rest of the summer with us and coming back anytime. The crew was willing, but some spoilsport in the office had plans to send them north, into the interior of British Columbia, where, tragically, Phil, the cook, was killed in the crash of a light plane.

Upon departure from Puffin Cove, the crew left behind plywood and other materials that were uneconomical to fly out and ship to the next camp. That seems to be the way in the north country—spend the money to move it in; save money by not taking it out. We were happy to have everything they left and knew exactly how we would use it. We would build an additional room onto the cabin—a cooking and dining room. Once the room was built, however, I claimed it as my writing room.

Of course the prospectors never told us if they found anything. But so far as Betty and I were concerned, their time in Puffin Cove had been a great success.

The Texas Gulf Sulfur crew left Puffin Cove one day, and we shoved off the next for Sandspit.

Unfortunately, no one had stolen Betty's whale. Our grandson and I were drafted into assisting Betty. Gene and Patty worked on the house and yard and prepared our meals.

There was no shortage of advice—all free and worth its price. Apparently everyone had seen movies taken at whale factories, afloat or ashore. We had only a few offers of assistance, and they were gratefully accepted. I soon found my sheath knife to be the best tool available. Whales reduced aboard factory ships or stations are hauled from the sea and up clean ramps. On board, razor-sharp flensing knives quickly cut through blubber, flesh, and tendons. This whale had rolled on beaches until the blubber was impregnated with sand and fine gravel. One short slice, and my knife was dull. I spent a lot of time with a file and sharpening stone.

Skeletonizing is slow, smelly, solitary labor. Sightseers often stood upwind uttering the predictable "How can you stand it?" while we worked—up to our elbows—in slippery blubber and rotting meat.

"It's like wading into cold water," I would reply. "You're tempted to get out. It's not half bad if you dive in. By now we're used to the smell."

We wanted to see the massive heart. Was the whale pregnant? Would we find clues to the cause of death?

A whale depends on the surrounding water to cool its body. Ashore on warm summer days, the dark skin and thick blubber not only absorbed heat but seemed to insulate and maintain that heat, literally cooking the organs. That soupy interior told us nothing.

"Of course we'd rather work on a fresh carcass," Betty explained to friends, "but we're just lucky to have *any* whale so close to home to learn from."

We have always questioned the evolutionary theory of "vestigial hipbones." According to the theory, whales were originally land mammals that moved to the sea, lost their legs and developed flippers. We found those bones. Their location and connecting muscles seem more consistent with their purpose as described in one of our many books on whales—as anchors for muscles around the sex organs.

One day I asked a friend, Harold Bronsch, to help strip off a blanket of blubber with his four-wheel-drive jeep. "Sure, if you have a two-hundred-foot rope," he said. We did. Harold showed up wearing a World War II gas mask.

We tagged, numbered, and labeled the bones before trucking them to our yard, where they cured for over a year. Fortunately, there were many vacant lots between us and the nearest neighbors.

After over two weeks of work, we were nearly finished. The heavy skull was winched into the pickup, trucked home, and set up where maggots could do the final cleanup. Not aesthetically pleasing, but most effective. We learned afresh what biologists have known for a long time—maggots clean bones completely and without damage.

Clothes and boots went into the fireplace. After two or three shampoos and as many showers, we were ready to rejoin human society.

After this unusual experience, Betty and I were able to make a small contribution to the International Whale Symposium at the University of Indiana in 1975. So far we have articulated only one flipper out of all the bones stored in our large garage. The remainder of the skeleton is an assembly job to keep us busy some winter when we can't be out on *Skylark* or at Puffin Cove.

13

Arrow Post Cruise

Betty and I sat in the small galley of the Fisheries Patrol Vessel *Arrow Post* with Captain Barney Kinnie, who had sailed the old windjammers. As we were leaving, Barney said, "Why don't you both come out with us next week when we check the herring spawn and open the halibut season?" A smile washed across his weathered face. "We won't be gone more than ten days. Be back by May second."

I glanced at Betty. She appeared interested. "Thanks, Barney. That's the best offer we've had in years. But we just got back from a winter in Gardner Canal as watchmen at a logging camp, and there's a million things I should be doing."

"Go ahead, Neil," Betty said enthusiastically. "There's nothing that can't wait. As for *Skylark,* I'll stay and check it every few days."

Betty had met Barney in Butedale when she was returning to Puget Sound from Alaska in her dugout and Barney's vessel nearly swamped her in a narrow passage. I met him later, when he was transferred to the Charlottes.

Arrow Post's husky diesel was warming up when I climbed over the gunwale. Although she was far from new, Barney and his crew cared for her like a family heirloom.

The crew was in the galley. "Just having a final cup," was Barney's greeting. "Grab one for yourself." I filled a mug. "Do you know everybody?"

"Not the engineer." It was a simple matter of elimination to figure out the position of the strong-shouldered man with dark eyes and hair sprinkled with gray.

"That's Jack. He's relief engineer. Jimmy's off this trip." We shook hands.

"Morning, Alf. Hi, Andy," I said to the mate and cook. Alf was stocky, with a well-cared-for stomach. Glasses didn't hide the fact that one of Andy's eyes didn't function.

Alfred Moody, the barrel-chested Haida mate, pointed out his newly painted home as we passed Skidegate Mission. The late April sun was bright and warm. Three of us were wedged into the ridiculously small pilot house, trying to guess what the weather was going to do.

Barney had the wheel. He tapped the barometer with a nicotine-stained finger. "Thing's been dancin' up and down faster than a fiddler's elbow. Radio says the southeaster's blown over. Looks like they guessed right for once." As Barney steered, he bent his six-foot-plus frame so his head wouldn't hit the overhead.

The fifty-five-foot *Arrow* corkscrewed as we turned south into Hecate Strait. Barney kept the seas broad on our port bow. Alf and I braced ourselves. The wind dropped to ten knots, but the waves still washed over the boat and sloshed down the decks.

"I'll check things on deck," Alf said. He was trapped in the pilot house until I stepped outside.

Just then Andy tumbled out of the galley and heaved a pan of something white and stringy over the side.

"Okay, Andy?" Alf asked, peering into the galley. There was a strong smell of burned coffee, and streaks of drying coffee covered the white enamel stove.

"Damn boat's no place to cook!" Andy growled. "Tell Barney chow will be a little late. Spaghetti jumped off the stove."

Arrow's three boats and many drums of fuel were lashed down in a manner to keep Alf happy.

By afternoon the sea was flat. On Tanu Island a few weary totems gazed up at us. Some leaned at improbable angles; the next strong wind might push them over.

"My people came from there," Alf said, breaking the silence. There was pride and sadness in his soft voice. He stared at the desolate village, seeing things not visible to Barney or me.

Although Tanu was abandoned nearly a quarter-century before Alf's birth, the sight of it evoked memories of his childhood. "My parents were fishing at Burnaby Island. I was a little boy." A wistful smile lit Alf's handsome face. "My uncle and I left to go home to Skidegate in his thirty-foot dugout. A southeaster blew up. Got worse fast. Uncle kept throwing things overboard. Even dumped out the big bear he's snared."

A bear was important to the Haidas and not easy to come by. It meant food, fat to cook with, sinew for sewing, and a warm fur robe for the bed.

"Finally we landed at Copper Bay. A bad trip!" Alf's large, dark eyes crinkled. "Still don't know how we got home in that dugout."

Alf was born during especially difficult years for the Natives. Disease had cut their numbers to the lowest in history. Then the government decided that the Indians should abandon their ways and adopt the white man's ways. Alf, like many other boys and girls, was sent from his village to a distant boarding school.

"I learned English and forgot my own language. When I

came home, I couldn't talk with my parents." This was one of the few times I ever saw Alf anything but happy. "We learned to milk cows." Now he smiled. "I always thought milk came from tin cans. We had to pull it from those cows. And what good did it do me?"

His point was valid. Milk cows require regular care and chores that do not fit the mobile, seasonal life of Indians.

"I wanted to learn how to hunt and fish. Things that would do me good. One summer I came home and my father was dead. I never had a chance to know him."

Over the years, Betty and I met many Natives who had attended the government boarding schools, where a new culture was instilled. These men and women were leaders in their villages, respected members of their bands or tribes—positions earned at a high price.

Alf completed school, forgot about cows, and then quickly learned how to mend a net, fillet a salmon, and gut a halibut. His keen brown eyes studied the sky, the wind, the sea, a compass, a barometer, and charts. Soon he was captain of a money-making fishing boat.

"We'll stay at the water hole tonight," Barney announced. The water hole is a notch in Moresby Island along Hoya Passage and opposite Shuttle Island with an all-tide deep-water moorage. A plastic hose carries frigid water to the float from a falls hidden behind a jagged promontory.

No sooner were we tied up than Alf was over the side to grab the hose. He playfully washed down the decks and bulkheads before topping off the freshwater tanks.

"Hey, Alf, there's a big bear out here!" Jack yelled. "There, by the stiffleg." We scrambled out of the mess to look. Twice that day Alf had asked if anyone had seen a bear. No one had. "Not good. Somebody should have seen one by now. Been a hard winter," he reminded us.

Now a relieved smile crossed his leathery face. "He's after little crabs for supper. Let's eat too."

The next morning chill wind flooded the pilot house before Alf could slam the door behind him. "That wind's sharper than a filleting knife!" His hunched, broad shoulders were padded with a thick, hand-knitted wool sweater. "No spring this year. Nothing but cold."

There were no gulls hovering or fighting around the kelp beds in Sedgwick Bay. "Not much spawn this year," Alf said sadly. "Herring's fished out." He and his people depended on nature's bounty for a share of their food. Gathering and preparing it was always family work and family fun; everyone from toddlers to grandparents participated.

"Maybe we can do a little jigging," Alf said hopefully.

Barney didn't answer but just gazed out the window, eyeing some old snag or point ashore and sneaking an occasional peek at the fathometer's squiggly graph. Abruptly, Barney threw the clutch into neutral and then reverse. When the white water reached the bow, Barney moved the controls to neutral and the throttle to idle. *Arrow* lay dead in the water close to a charted reef off Faraday Island.

Alf and Jack had their jigs on the bottom before I could get to the fantail. "Got one," was Jack's laconic announcement as he hauled in a twenty-four-inch red snapper and swung it aboard.

Alf soon boated two lingcod; the larger was nearly three feet long. Alf and Jack had caught fish for the evening meal and also had some fun—all in less time than office workers take for a coffee break.

"Thar she blows!" Barney yelled in his best Captain Ahab voice.

We were just south of Ramsay Island, in the wide, southern entrance to Juan Perez Sound. Barney pointed to a ruffled spot on the sea. At least a minute slowly ticked by before steaming vapor erupted. Seconds later there was another spout. Then a whale broached, showing its rough, rounded back and, far aft, a small dorsal fin.

"Gray whales," Alf said, after we had watched a few minutes. "See them migrating every spring and fall." He was happy. Seeing these whales, like seeing the bear, assured Alf that all was right with nature.

Alf had an inexhaustible collection of Haida stories. There was no guessing what might trigger one. Now he pointed to a rust-colored bluff on the north side of Hutton Inlet. "Used to be a village there. Killer from another village came in and shot the chief's nephew with a strong bow."

Alf didn't have to tell us that the nephew had been next in line to become chief. He gave us a stern look. "Know what they did?"

"Killed him," Barney and I said.

"Tied him up and burned him!"

"And I'll bet they didn't waste a second about it or have any lengthy appeals," I said as Alf stepped out of the pilot house.

"Maybe now you know why I call this the *Haida Post*," Barney said half seriously. "Almost always there's two Haidas in the crew, sometimes three. All I hear about are the bears and the eagles and the old people."

And I knew he enjoyed every moment of it.

Skincuttle Inlet was calm. Cumulus clouds wandered across the sky. Barney tapped the barometer one more time. "Seems to be holding steady. We'll slip around and into Louscoone this afternoon."

As we swung past Harriet Harbour, Alf jabbed a stubby finger toward the kelp beds surrounding the point. "Gulls! The herring are spawning." Glaucous-winged gulls and other sea birds were congregating, dipping their heads under the surface to tear at the kelp leaves. Some gulls hovered a few feet above; then folded their wings and dove into the spawn area. The air was filled with milling, mewling, feeding birds, each expressing displeasure at having to share.

"Bet the herring have just started to spawn," Barney said.

"We'll check this out on the way back. See how much the birds leave."

Two female sea lions popped up near the port side, took a quick, long-necked look, and settled under the water.

The seas lapped gently at the worn headlands along Hecate Strait. Barney and Alf told me how *Arrow* is used for rescue, salvage, scientific research, and experimental fishing as well as for patrol.

Betty and I sometimes met people who had been helped or befriended by *Arrow Post's* crew. Only two winters before, friends of ours were rescued by the *Arrow* after ditching their amphibious de Havilland Beaver in Hecate Strait when they ran out of fuel during a rising southeaster.

Nearly eight miles of flat, calm water lay ahead of us as we entered Louscoone Inlet. Andy began preparing the evening meal as comfortably as if he were ashore.

"Boundary markers are okay," Alf reported, returning the binoculars to their box, after checking the white triangles nailed to trees on each side of the inlet.

We anchored in front of the fishery guardian's cabin. Two ricks of stove wood were piled near the doorway. The place looked ready for occupancy—just as soon as the bucket covering the chimney was removed.

Alf and I decided to go ashore and have a look at the cabin. Kindling and firewood lay near the cabin stove, its door open to permit circulation of air, its top protected by a layer of lard, and its sides coated with oil. An airtight glass jar held dry matches. Tea, sugar, beans, flour, and a few other staples were also stored in glass containers on the shelf. There was an old but clean set of clothes. Enough for any survivor or lost hunter. Blankets hung across a stainless steel wire stretched high across the room. All this spoke of a woodsman's care and attention to numerous small yet important details.

Alf rowed along the shore while I walked, picking up lumber that had washed in during the winter. Alf was building a garage and needed a few more pieces. Here, in these tree-burdened islands, lumber is outlandishly expensive.

A young seal followed close behind the boat, bobbing up for a quick peek and then dropping straight down, closing its wide nostrils just as it submerged. Alf whistled and the seal reappeared, swimming about thirty feet astern. Could Alf really communicate with wildlife? It seemed so.

Sometime during the night I was awakened by the steady rapping of rain on the wooden deck above my bunk. It ceased before dawn. When I stepped out on deck in the morning's dim light, we were enveloped in clinging fog. It looked like the dirty cotton waste used by an engineer to wipe up his bilges.

The tide was low when *Arrow* anchored near an unnamed islet west of Rose Harbour. Herring had spawned here, and gulls were fighting for the bounty. We launched the speedboat, and Alf and I planed away toward the kelp.

When we reached the kelp, Alf heaved a small grapnel into it. Retrieving the kelp-covered hooks, he tore off a few leaves sprinkled with a frosting of spawn. "Fresh spawn. Three, maybe four days old," he announced after looking, feeling, and sniffing.

Barney told me that Alf was an expert on herring spawn, "Even knows more about it than the herring!" I believe it. Alf maneuvered the boat around, pulling in more samples, checking the thickness and percentage of leaves covered. "Everything eats herring spawn—gulls, eagles, crows, even Indians," Alf laughed as we moved away. "And now the Japs want to buy the roe before it's spawned!"

Alf leaned over the side, his face nearly in the water. "Real low tide. Might as well get some abs." In a moment he was prying abalone from the boulders covering the bottom, while I poled the boat and kept it off the rocks. In a few moments we had our limit. This was something else he hadn't learned in school at Coqualeetza.

"Look! A herring ball!" Barney pointed across *Arrow's*

starboard bow. "Where those gulls and eagles are circling." He spun the helm to starboard.

Gulls were hungrily diving. Surfacing with a herring, a bird would twist the wriggling fish around until it could be swallowed headfirst. Eagles swooped low, yellow legs thrust forward, wings and tail feathers spread wide to brake their dives. Usually they would rise with a fish and fly off to the nearest tree or beach to feed.

Arrow circled the roe-filled herring. There were tons of them, slowly moving, not in a school side by side, but in a dense mass some twenty-five feet across and probably as deep. Safety in numbers? Evidently. But those on top were being eaten by birds. And any fish, seal, sea lion, or whale could dash in and really make a killing.

"That ball might contain more herring than a seine boat could carry," Barney informed me. "I've seen a boat make a set and catch more than it could hold. Skipper just radioed the packer to come alongside and take them. One set like that can make a good season for any herring fisherman. Doubt if I'll ever see it again." Barney sounded wistful. "Herring seem to be disappearing. Maybe it's only a cycle. Nobody seems to know."

We arrived at the Dolomite Narrows an hour before high tide, so we laid to in adjacent Bag Harbour. A gaggle of Canada geese took flight. "Probably homesteaders," Alf guessed. "Some of these geese never leave the Charlottes."

On the north shore a rusted boiler lay atop a pile of clamshells. Long before World War II the Japanese operated a small cannery here. Those were the years when the Japanese knew the Charlottes better than Canadian hydrographers.

Alf was at the helm when we entered the narrows. He and Barney leaned over the dodger as we eased through the rock-strewn Dolomites. Watching them, one might think they had all the room of the vast Pacific to maneuver in and at least one hundred fathoms under the keel. Actually, we were within

145

spitting distance of rocks on either beam and had no more than two feet of water under the keel.

The land and sea appeared deserted. Then midway across Juan Perez Sound we sighted a vessel hull down in Hecate Strait—a tug departing the Charlottes towing two barges piled high with logs for mainland mills. The early explorers used to encounter more people than we did. Two hundred years ago there were about eight thousand Haidas here. Now there were about thirteen hundred Haidas and enough Caucasians to bring the population to about five thousand people.

Dusk was closing around us when *Arrow* tied up at the water hole. Once more Alf whipped the hose over the boat before filling the water tanks.

Silent, opalescent fog held us in a damp cocoon the next morning when I swung open the double doors of the after cabin and clambered on deck. The near shore—twenty-five feet distant—loomed through a silvery haze. Astern, across Hoya Passage, Shuttle Island no longer existed.

Tanu, the department's newest and largest patrol and experimental fishing vessel, was calling *Arrow* before we backed away from the float.

Barney smelled our way along the narrow passage, head and left shoulder thrust out the pilot house window. Swiveling this way and that, pinched nostrils breathing in moist air, he groped along the near but unseen shore. By perceiving the nearly indistinguishable differences in fog density, listening for the barely discernible slap of a wave against a tidal rock, and judging the time required for the echo of *Arrow's* whistle to return, Barney guided us safely north toward Lockeport.

Visibility improved as the fog slowly turned to soggy mist. As Barney said after pulling in his head and reaching for his tin of "makin's," "Any change would have to be for the better!" He deftly rolled a cigarette and snapped it to his lips.

Arrow was lying to—stopped and drifting to any land-lubber—off Lockeport. Barney was slugging down another

146

coffee. The mist on our starboard bow became darker and more solid. Like watching an artist create a charcoal drawing, we watched a large gray ship gradually materialize. It was heading directly for us, gray on gray. There was no other color until her port running light, a dim, misty red, peeked through.

Tanu turned parallel and stopped alongside, with six or eight feet of gray water between us. She loomed high overhead. Her main deck was above *Arrow's* pilot house. *Tanu's* radar antenna was rotating steadily. *Arrow's* was not working. "The ability to get where you're going without radar," Barney told me as we hauled away from the float that morning, "is the vital difference between an old seaman and a new mariner."

Barney and the captain of *Tanu* held a conflab about herring, halibut, and *Tanu's* experimental trapping of sablefish (Alaska black cod). Collapsible steel cages four feet square and thirty inches deep covered *Tanu's* broad afterdeck. This was a new concept in fishing. Only fish of a predetermined size could be held within the trap—alive and fresh—whenever the traps were lifted. An obvious improvement over indiscriminate hooks, especially in foul weather when it is impossible to haul in the gear for days and the hooked fish are often dead or destroyed by bottom-dwelling scavengers, identified by fishermen as "live bottom."

After ten minutes of gamming, *Tanu's* whistle blasted our ears and she slipped away, disappearing into the light rain. *Arrow* turned north, toward home.

The late afternoon sun bounced off a half-dozen aluminum-sided trailers when we turned into Thurston Harbour. One side of the bay was filled with logs. A large truck was stopped under a sturdy A-frame made of two thick spruce sticks. Water splashed high as the load of logs was dropped into the salt chuck. The empty trailer was hoisted atop the tractor and, with a burst of black smoke, it rumbled away for another load.

Halibut boats, two and three deep, rimmed the float,

nearly hiding the logging tug. Barney eased alongside a boom stick, and we tied up. Ashore, a freshly painted sign welcomed us to Thurston Harbour and the Frank Beban Logging Company. This was the company Betty and I had worked for as watchmen from late October to mid-April in Gardner Canal, on the mainland. A precut home, trailers for families, and a small bed of flowers nestled among a grove of trees overlooking the entrance. A repair shop, storage area, and tank farm completed the campsite.

The next morning I was awakened by the sound of the fishermen's boats getting underway. It was black outside. I tucked in for another hour. *Arrow Post's* crew might be watching the fishermen, but we didn't have to keep fishermen's long hours.

After another of Andy's excellent breakfasts, we got underway. It was not quite eight o'clock. We patrolled to the east, past Reef Island, where countless gulls, cormorants, terns, and other sea birds were busy claiming and fighting for nesting spots.

The halibuters had their gear in the water to "soak," marked by large red floats and red flags waving from long, upright bamboo poles. They would have a few hours to wait before hauling in the first set to learn if the skipper had chosen a good spot, or if there were any halibut. Each year the catch seemed to be declining. More days of fishing were required to fill the icy holds. What could be done? Would a hatchery help, as it had helped salmon? One fisherman suggested that a ten-year moratorium—throughout the world—on fishing halibut would give them a chance to propagate. That was one of the most unpopular ideas I had heard in years. Let's pray it doesn't have to come to that!

Late in the afternoon we headed into Cumshewa Inlet and on to Beattie Anchorage, where we moored to one of the buoys for the night.

This had been a successful cruise. Alf, Jack, and Andy

each had several pounds of choice lingcod and red snapper fillets to take home; Alf now had nearly enough beachcombed lumber to complete his garage; from Barney, the Fisheries Department would receive a concise report concerning the herring spawn; and I had learned more about Canada's great fishing industry and was reassured that specialists were striving to enhance this valuable and renewable resource.

14

February Hurricane

It was mid-February and we were heading out for our third day at sea. We had delayed this trip for too long; the reasonably calm and cold winter weather had begun to turn windy and wet early in February.

We had left Sandspit in September, enjoying a cruise down Moresby's east coast and up the west to Puffin Cove. We spent October close to the cabin, for that month is likely to include one or more wild storms. In November and December we ranged to the nearest bays and inlets, fishing, hunting, or photographing. We had also made two trips to Tasu for mail and supplies, being lucky enough to have smooth seas both ways as a result of the prevailing northeast winds that blow for a week or more at a time from November through February.

During these extended periods of calm seas, which were as quiet as the seas during the summer, we would get in our wood supply. We rolled logs down the steep outer beach at low tide and then rounded them up with the small boat as they drifted off during high tide. After rigging lines on one to four logs at a time, we would tow them into Puffin Cove, tying them near the steps to the cabin, where, at low tide, I could chain saw them into firewood.

We had not picked up mail and provisions since the week before Christmas. We had planned to do so before now, but we were delayed by nearly ten days of southerly storms. Then it calmed—some.

We weren't out of food—with an abundance of fish and venison, we would never starve—but our variety was certainly limited, and some fresh fruit and vegetables would be a treat. Worst of all, I had finished the last of our three-pound tins of peanut butter two weeks earlier. To me, that was a crisis. We were also wondering how our sons and their families and our mothers were. Betty's mother was in her late eighties; mine, a decade younger.

Now we were coming out of Blue Heron Bay—our last possible shelter—into a rising southeaster of thirty to thirty-five knots. This trip had become an endurance contest as we crept from inlet to inlet. First we stopped in Mike and Barry inlets for short respites from the long northwest swells overlain with waves from the southwest. Then we went into Pocket Inlet to replenish our wood supply and get a night's rest before going on to Sunday Inlet and finally Blue Heron Bay for our second night.

"Even the sea lions are smart enough to take shelter." I pointed at the colony of about a hundred Steller's sea lions, their fat bodies speckling a wide and sloping rock.

Before we reached Tasu Head, a steady forty-five knots of wind was raising the sea, ripping the crests off breaking waves eight to ten feet high, and casting them in long lines of foaming spindrift. Wind, sea, and tide were going with us, and double-ended *Skylark* scudded along at well over her usual six knots. We were rolling and pitching but not pounding.

Rounding the bare islet at Tasu Head, we turned into the

"gap"—the narrow, deep, and steep-sided opening to Tasu Sound. Wind and rain now funneled between the high, bald headlands at some sixty knots. This was no problem today, however, because the sharp mountainsides deflected some of the wind downward, holding the water nearly flat as both wind and sea rushed into the extensive sound. Had the tide been ebbing instead of flooding, it would have been a different matter. Wind and water would have been battling, creating high choppy seas, attacking any vessel from every direction.

"I'm going below to build a fire," Betty said, "and get into some dry clothes." We had taken a nasty wave over the gunwale just outside Blue Heron Bay, and she was cold.

All but three of the fifty to sixty boats belonging to the mine employees were hauled out, secure in the lee of homes or apartments. Those smart boat owners wouldn't have to crawl out in the middle of a stormy night to check on their craft. So finding a place to tie up was no problem for us. We moored between two thick logs jutting from under the heavy, decked-over float.

Few people moved about the townsite. The crew going on the afternoon shift took shelter under the bunkhouse breeze-way while awaiting the small shuttle bus to the mine.

The wind continued to build. By dusk—about five o'clock—it was bending the trees, snapping the flag flying in the townsite square, and howling and whistling across the dock and between the building at eighty knots—a fair hurricane in the Charlottes. Short, fast waves raced toward us in Hunger Harbour. Wind shot across the low causeway, tearing at tarps covering the supplies stored there.

Fat raindrops hammered *Skylark's* cabin and decks throughout the night. Our boat strained and jerked at her mooring lines, though she rode safely in the lee of the float, squeaking noisily as her metal sides rubbed against the old tires nailed to the logs as fenders. We were warm and comfortable, thankful to have reached this haven.

The rain ceased before a pale sun climbed the surrounding mountains next morning. The wind dropped; the barometer rose. Hunger Harbour was once more flat.

The amphibious feeder plane from Sandspit couldn't get in because of zero visibility in the intervening mountain passes. Flight reservations from Sandspit to Vancouver and beyond were canceled; vacations and appointments, delayed. Incoming employees scurried around Sandspit and Queen Charlotte City trying to find hotel rooms and a place to eat.

Conditions were no better the following day. Low clouds continued to roam the hillsides, cutting off anything above 250 feet. It was not an uncommon winter condition.

Passengers and mail from Sandspit were transported by van to the abandoned Moresby Camp at the head of Cumshewa Inlet, then by cabin cruiser to the logging camp at Sewell Inlet, and again by van across seven miles of logging road to Newcombe Inlet in Tasu Sound, where they were piled into a boat for the final leg of their four- to five-hour trip home. (This would be a twenty-five-minute trip by air). Picking up our mail, we learned that all was well with our families. After posting our replies and picking up provisions at the co-op store, we were underway.

Long, easy-riding northwest swells made our return trip a pleasure. "Guess winter's worst storms are over," I said. It was the nineteenth of February.

We were happy to be back in the quiet beauty of Puffin Cove. The cabin was warm by the time *Skylark* was unloaded.

"I'll go fishing tomorrow," I told Betty that evening, "or if it's really nice, we might go to Two Buck Bay for a deer." We had not bagged one since before Christmas, and we were hungry for a good venison roast. The season would close at the end of the month, and I had one more deer tag. Any day we could look out the windows and see one to seven deer browsing on washed-up kelp leaves around the lagoon. But they were our friends, and we never shot them.

A boisterous wind rushing through the tall spruce trees outside our open window roused me during the night, reminding me to repair the radio antenna swinging along the cabin's shake sides like a scratchy pendulum.

With the fire lit and the coffee pot on, I had time to check the thermometer; it was up to a comfortable 43° Fahrenheit. Then the barometer; it was down to a disquieting 28.7 inches—and still dropping. Occasionally local storms come and go with little change in barometric pressure. When the barometer drops below 29.3 inches, I'm ready to believe we are due for dirty weather—and soon.

Low black clouds rudely jostled each other, merging and dividing as mountain passes confused the rising wind. At times gusts moved in opposite directions as they whipped around a point, butted against a tree-covered hillside, and bounced off on a reverse course. After watching the sea, I concluded the wind was coming from the southwest.

Tumbling white-maned rollers bashed against the bare granite boulders surrounding the lagoon's entrance, breaking into frothy fans before flying thirty to fifty feet up and blasting into the stunted, twisted trees, where, for a few minutes, the froth stuck like cotton candy. There would be no fishing or hunting today.

The wind's moan gradually increased to a violent roar. Trees leaned at disquieting angles. Spray and scud flew farther than any pitcher ever threw a baseball. Clouds moved faster than the fleetest sprinter. The noise of the sea climbed decibel by decibel.

The sea changed from charcoal gray to light green as the surface water became aerated. Gusts were furious. Our cabin trembled.

We hiked through the moaning forest and a narrow gulch to the outside beach, where drift logs, accumulated over the years, were piled ten to fifteen feet deep. High tide and crashing breakers washed logs in and out, tumbling them end over end, rolling, battering, splintering, and restacking logs and rocks. We were witnessing an infinitesimal portion of the unmeasured and unharnessed energy of wind and water.

The surrounding mountainsides were getting a good washdown. Each small declivity became a rivulet. Trickles became streams. Streams were now raging, frothing torrents. All flooded into the lagoon, changing its beautiful green water to the color of strong coffee. This dark water met the light green salt water at the restricted entrance, and they fought—one to get in; the other to get out. Probably the flood tide did enter; otherwise the lagoon might have been like a rising dam, with fresh water from the streams filling it as fast as the tide rose.

Small limbs broke and flew away. The spirelike top of an old snag snapped. Water was scooped from the lagoon and hurled into the wind with a twisting motion. I stood upright with difficulty when I went outside to get a few shots with my underwater camera. The wind was backing to the south, perhaps the southeast. It was blowing at least eighty knots—a real force thirteen hurricane—and still building.

I checked my watch; it was two o'clock.

In my room, where we have on oil heater, gusts blew down the cloverleaf chimney, blasting greasy soot and acrid fumes out the damper, reminding me of Los Angeles smog. "I'm quitting for the day," I told Betty, who was typing in the main cabin.

"Good. Maybe you can get some heat out of this stove. The wood is burning, but there's no warmth."

She had the draft and damper closed. Yet that wind was drawing nearly all the heat up and out the Yukon chimney.

Our ten-foot skiff is kept on a continuous line below the cabin, where a large rock gives it some protection. The wind was increasing as the tide ebbed. I checked the boat again. It had overturned. The stern was propped up by the outboard, and the fuel tank had tumbled up on the beach, tethered by its hose. A pike pole was on the sand. Both oars and a spare paddle were where we had put them—safely lashed to the seat.

I had made a small grid, above high water, to stow the boat on during bad weather. This seemed like a time to use it, although I wondered why I hadn't done it sooner. In a few minutes I was soaked, but the boat was tied to the grid and out of the wind.

The storm continued to increase. Our cabin shook. Wind plucked at the heavy fishnet hanging over a log crossing a gully, holding it nearly horizontal. The brown grass was plastered against the ground.

When the tide was nearly out, we decided to walk around and check on *Skylark*. The ferocious wind was hurling water, sand, kelp, small broken branches, and anything else that was loose. Sand was embedded in the rockweed, turning its normally slippery surface into a nonskid walkway.

Three mallards—a duck and two drakes—leaped into the wind, wings beating frantically. At first it looked as though they were double-timing in place. Then we realized they were going backwards. As we watched in amazement, they gave up the fight and splashed into the water; then they sought refuge among the boulders.

Farther along the crescent-shaped lagoon we scared up a family of mergansers. They all took off with the wind except one drake. He tried to but was knocked down with a splash and paddled for shore.

Rounding the point where the river otters sometimes play and slide on the rocks, we came upon two snapped-off trees lying in the lagoon. I was waiting for Betty near one when the muffled honk of a Canada goose sounded nearby. Five of these magnificent birds staggered through the air like combat-damaged aircraft whose stabilization and elevation controls no longer functioned. One was buffeted by a weighty gust and plummeted to within fifteen feet of us as it put on full power to maintain flight and pass over.

Never before had we realized how much trouble a storm could be to God's creatures. Small birds, deer, and other land animals stayed somewhere deep within the shelter of the forest or the land's irregular valleys and gulches.

Skylark was riding the choppy waves nicely, tugging easily at her mooring lines and rubbing against the tires rimming the fifty-foot float rigged against a concave cliff.

By now the storm was up to a steady 100 knots and gusting to 125. Fortunately, we do not often experience anything over 100 knots. I had to draw on a winter at sea in the Gulf of Alaska, riding a tanker along the Aleutians, plus leaning out into the slipstream of an aircraft while shooting pictures to recall the sharp press of skin against bone and the uncomfortable stretch of the eyelids.

Wind continued to tumble and roll down the mountains, squeeze through the narrow passes, and shoot across the lagoon, sweeping up water and sand. Sheets of salt water washed against the cabin, across the roof, and down the lee side. Water cascaded down the double windows; it was as though we were driving through a car wash.

"This is the first time I've ever been ashore and felt the sensation of being at sea," I told Betty. The cabin is about twenty feet above normal high tide.

"I'm thankful this hurricane and a spring tide didn't coincide," Betty replied.

The storm blew itself out after dusk. The cabin was snug. Our prayers for safety were answered. We slept.

The next morning we heard on the radio that Cape St. James had reported gusts in excess of 100 knots and that Sandspit Airport had experienced winds over 103 knots. (Anemometers at both places are calibrated to only 100 knots.) Later one of the men on duty at the airport told me, "The needle on the anemometer tried to wrap itself around the peg when some of those gusts hit!"

The morning was cold. A fuliginous sky spit icy needles.

The wind was down to a reasonable twenty-five knots. We hiked around the lagoon and outside beach. Many trees were roughly pruned; others were toppled. The great collection of logs on the outer beach was bright and splintery from grinding against the rocks. Washtub-size rocks were rearranged in sharp, upswept windrows. Smaller rocks of five to fifteen pounds had been tossed up on top of the pile of logs.

Red rockfish were washed ashore, churned up from the ocean bottom, along with many small red, yellow, and white sponges. On one beach we discovered a storm petrel, apparently drowned.

Now we include February with October as the months most likely to have violent storms—storms whose beauty and ferocity can only be appreciated by seeing them—storms that teach us always to seek a safe anchorage if we hope to become senior citizens.

15

Salvaging an Anchor

It was late in March when Bill Hill, pilot for Okanagan Helicopters, dropped by to visit us. He had been flying around the Charlottes evaluating the feasibility of establishing a base in Sandspit. We talked about beachcombing, World War II, Coast Watch cabins, and the wrecked *Clarksdale Victory*. Then Bill threw us a curve. "What do you know about the old shipwreck just north of Kindakun Point?"

Betty and I glanced at each other and simultaneously asked, "What wreck?" We thought we knew the coast. We had been ashore at Kindakun Point and Cone Head, but we had not walked the intervening two miles of uninteresting bouldery beach.

Bill could only tell us there was a large anchor and some pieces that were probably from an old sailing ship. We were immediately anxious to check it out.

April was a wild, unsettled month. When the weather improved in early May, Betty and I headed west, through

Skidegate Narrows. Birds were singing, courting, and nesting. Spring had arrived.

The sea leaped and snapped as we rounded Hunter Point's long reef; we wouldn't be landing on any coastal beach today. A strong westerly swell rolled into Kano Inlet, lifting and tossing us until we turned into Givenchy Anchorage, at the inlet's head. Snow-covered mountains loomed above, sheltering us from the wind but obliterating the warm spring sun.

Each morning for the next five days we went out as far as Cadman Island, sometimes to Kindakun Point, before being driven back by heavy seas.

Finally the barometer crept upward, and the wind and waves died down. We rounded the point and headed north, holding close to the jumbled rocks, where long rollers washed up the gravel beach.

"There's a lead!" *Skylark* rolled uneasily as we studied the desolate coast of black volcanic rock. Lowering the binoculars, I pointed. "Just to the right of those tall twin rocks."

Betty watched a half-dozen waves roll in. "Yes, it's the only place."

If anyone could land there, Betty could. I launched the fiberglass skiff. Betty hopped in and untied the oars and spare paddle.

"I won't be long." Betty always promised that. She and I just had different definitions of "long."

Betty paused outside the low breakers, catching the wave's rhythm. Then between waves, she rowed quickly into the slim lead. She leaped ashore, dragged the boat up on the wash from the next wave, and kicked the small anchor into the gravel. Her boots weren't even wet.

Skylark jogged for well over an hour while Betty searched the shore. At last she returned, tossing a deadeye and a long bronze pin on deck before climbing aboard. Her hazel eyes sparkled like a kid's on Christmas morning. "That's it! There's a big anchor, chain, and more deadeyes. Anchor's underwater in a slot in the reef."

"If this weather holds, we'll try to get ashore tomorrow on the rising tide and I can get some pictures." We were returning to Givenchy Anchorage, and the sea was calming.

We were underway at dawn. Two hours later we anchored offshore from the wreck. The sea was rolling easily; there were no breaking waves.

I mounted the outboard and we zipped ashore. Betty led me to the anchor, which stood on edge in a tapered crevice filled with water. The stock and one fluke were hidden under a layer of gravel. The anchor had a curved piece on the back of each fluke, unlike any I had ever seen. We searched the area and found four more deadeyes, a futtock band, mast and spar hoops, and a pocket full of copper nails.

Betty returned from slogging through tall grass in a clearing above the high-tide line. "Been looking for any sign of survivors or a carved figurehead. A ship that size must have had one."

"What survivors are going to clear a half-acre? That's a natural clearing."

"I don't think so." Betty turned over a deadeye as if searching for a clue. "I wonder what its name was."

"For sure it's not listed on our wreck chart." I picked up two of the better deadeyes—circular, flat pieces of lignum vitae with three holes placed so that they looked like the eye sockets and nose of a skull and used as pulleys to adjust the tension on a ship's shrouds. Short lengths of spliced wire gripped their double-grooved edges. "Let's go home. There's nothing more we can learn here."

"Could we salvage that anchor?" Betty sounded dubious.

I expected the question. I was surprised she had waited nearly an hour to ask. "Sure. Lots of work and at least two, maybe three days of flat seas. There's plenty of logs around.

Getting them into position will be the tough part."

I had replaced the worn connecting shackle between our thirty-five-pound Danforth anchor and the chain. Now we headed into Queen Charlotte City to buy a new spare. Betty decided to take the opportunity to visit her friend Emma Wilson in the hospital.

Finished at the hardware store, I returned to the floats and boarded the *Arrow Post*. As usual, Captain Barney Kinnie was aboard. When I began to describe some of the fittings we had seen at the wreck, his eyes brightened. He immediately named them and explained their functions. As a fifteen-year-old boy, Barney had gone to sea on an old windjammer sailing between Vancouver and Sydney. Now, nearing retirement, he happily recalled those hard, exciting years. Skippering a patrol vessel was a living—better than being ashore—but it lacked the challenge of real ships.

Betty knew where to find me and came aboard bursting with information. "Sol knows about that ship!" She cried. "Sol's older half-brother, Isaac, found it in the spring of nineteen-three." Sol was Chief Solomon Wilson, a handsome and active Haida in his late eighties. Luckily, he had been at the hospital to see his wife, Emma.

"Sol was a young teenager when Isaac first sighted the wreck from a dugout canoe as he paddled home from his spring trap lines in Rennel Sound. Only the forward half was aground. Torn sails flapped from a canted mast. No one was aboard. The bosun's locker was filled with paint and other stores. And there *was* a figurehead—a beautiful lady in a white dress. The Indians tried to get it off, but they didn't have the tools." Betty smiled.

"Isaac got into an argument with other Haidas who wanted a share of the stores and paint. It was his find, and he'd have it all or nothing—so he set fire to the hull."

"No!" Barney groaned. "What a waste!" But Barney knew this Northwest Coast and had no trouble believing the simple story.

"How about her name? Did Sol remember that?"

"Of course!" Betty gave me one of those wifely glances that said: How could you doubt it? "It was named *Flora*. He also said her capstan was brought ashore at Skidegate, where they used it for years to pull boats out of the water for winter storage or overhaul."

The name and date were clues enough. We would just look it up in Lloyd's or the American Registry of Shipping the next time we left the Charlottes and had access to a good library. Simple.

We flew out in the fall. The Seattle Public Library was one of our first stops. Picking an armful of books off the shelf, we sat down and looked up *Flora*. There were dozens of *Floras*, but none of them could be the one wrecked on the Charlottes. Hours later we were no nearer an answer.

We tried the library in Tacoma. Then Portland, San Francisco, Los Angeles, Long Beach, and, finally, San Diego. All had many of the same registry books; yet each had one or more volumes we hadn't seen before.

Before leaving Portland, we had decided to include the name *Florence* in our search—and *Florence* it was. In San Diego we found records of a sailing ship of that name whose size, age, and date of disappearance matched those of our ship. Built in Bath, Maine, in 1877, she had sailed from Tacoma, Washington, in December 1902 with a load of coal for the Oahu Railroad in Hawaii. After being towed to Cape Flattery, at the entrance to Juan de Fuca Strait, by a steam tug, she was never seen again. *Florence* was listed as missing at sea, presumed lost.

We had solved part of the mystery. But what had happened to this fine ship with a reputation for reliability? What about her crew of nearly thirty experienced seamen? And where were the lifeboats and the stern half?

Solomon had got the name wrong. But who wouldn't after seventy years? His valuable information had enabled us, however, to identify the wreck. Later we drove to Bath, Maine, and looked over the builder's records and photographs of *Florence*. It was a sturdy ship with lovely lines and a beautiful lady figurehead, carved by the famous artist Colonel Sampson. The photos showed that same rare anchor.

Our winter's research was finished. Spring came and went. I was recovering rapidly from major surgery. While waiting to get into the hospital, I had visited our friends Sam and Anne in Garden Bay, a portion of Pender Harbour, on British Columbia's Sunshine Coast. Sam Lamont, owner-operator of a towing and salvage company, is one of those rare individuals who can do nearly anything—and do it well. Anne is an attractive and competent nurse by training and a sailor by choice.

After looking over our pictures and asking a few pertinent questions, Sam said, "It'll be a lead pipe cinch! We're coming to the Charlottes again this summer. We'll give you a hand salvaging that anchor."

It was July when Sam and Anne arrived in the Charlottes aboard their thirty-two-foot tug, *Vulture*. Sam phoned from Masset before setting out for a leisurely holiday of beach-combing along the west coast of Graham Island. "We'll give you a hand with that anchor," he again promised before hanging up as the operator signaled the end of his three minutes.

Those late July days were warm and quiet. We were anxious to take advantage of every hour of calm weather. Betty and I tried to figure out where *Vulture* might be—we'd go out and meet them.

Our older son George, his wife Becky, and our grandson George II were up from California for the summer. Becky didn't care much for bouncing around in *Skylark*, so she decided to stay in Sandspit with George II and plant a small garden; radishes might mature before fall.

We were coasting along the south side of Hunter Point when Betty spotted *Vulture* charging south around the reef. George turned *Skylark* on an intercepting course. "Betty, pour some used oil in the stove to make black smoke," I yelled before leaping atop the cabin and waving a bright orange signal flag.

Vulture continued straight for Skidegate Channel. We saw Sam sitting in a relaxed attitude at the wheel. Intent on his own course, he looked neither to starboard nor to port. Soon *Vulture* was out of sight. A surprised Becky and George II welcomed us home late that night.

"Got engine trouble," Sam screamed into the phone the next day from Queen Charlotte City. "Spent fifteen hundred dollars to have that engine overhauled by the so-called experts so we could have a trouble-free trip. It's worse now than when I took it in. Should have done it myself. Would have saved money and had it done right! Just no time to do it!"

Another week dragged past—windless days of marvelous sun and blue sky decorated with fair-weather cumulus clouds—before *Vulture* was ready for sea.

"We'll meet you in Carew Bay," I promised as *Vulture* and *Skylark* warmed up in Alliford Bay.

Vulture's anchor light reflected on the slumbering water when we entered the sandy bay and anchored. At dawn the swelling roar of a high-speed engine brought me out of a deep sleep. Then I recognized *Vulture's* powerful diesel roaring at full speed. She was alongside by the time I scrambled on deck.

"Ready to take a look at that anchor?" Sam barked. *Vulture* rolled gently. Before I could answer, *Vulture's* heavy wake overtook both boats, and we leaped madly. The violent movement awakened Betty and George—as I think Sam intended it to.

"I'm going with Sam and Anne," I called into the dark cabin.

"Wait! I want to go too," Betty said.

With one powerful arm, Sam jerked our fiberglass boat onto *Vulture's* stern alongside his aluminum skiff. Betty and George leaped aboard. *Vulture* charged out of the bay. Anne, smiling and cheerful, passed around mugs of steaming coffee.

Tired rollers slopped across glistening rocks near the site of the wreck. We lay about two hundred feet offshore. Anne released the heavy anchor.

We launched both boats. Betty and George led the way in ours, and I rode with Sam and Anne. Standing near the stern and pushing on the oars in doryman fashion, Sam thrust us fifteen to twenty feet shoreward with every stroke.

"This is my souvenir," Anne called within seconds of stepping ashore as she picked up a deadeye from the shifting gravel.

We picked up two more deadeyes before reaching the anchor. That's a remarkable testimonial for any wood a hundred years old that has been subject to a ship's fire and then tumbled and thrashed by wild tidal waters and blasted by driven sand for over seventy years.

We walked the serried reef that angled down into the sea until we reached the great anchor, which was held in a tidal crevice, only one broad fluke exposed, covered by still water. The top of the stock and its connecting ring emerged about six feet away. The crosspiece was missing; made of wood, it had undoubtedly been burned or destroyed by teredoes. Rusted chain stretched across the reef.

"We'll take a pull and see what happens," said Sam, leaping the crevice for a better look.

Sam stood aft of the wheelhouse, at the stern steering station, where he could watch the line and my signals. This lonely beach was no place to wrap a line around *Vulture's* propeller. The tug was aligned with the crevice. I waved. The snaking line straightened out and stretched taut, water spraying from its straining strands. Suddenly the anchor stood upright— for only an instant; then it splashed onto the opposite side. Sam instantly threw the clutch into neutral.

168

The tide was flooding—time to do some serious thinking if we were going to salvage the anchor today. This calm was rare; it might be weeks before we could land here again. By then *Vulture* would be back at work among the Gulf Islands.

"Okay," Sam said, "we'll wrap two boom chains around the anchor and shackle them."

I agreed before I found out that was to be my job. I unenthusiastically stripped and jumped into the chilling, five-foot-deep water. Ten minutes later the chains were shackled and beachcombed plastic buoys attached to Sam's satisfaction.

Like most beaches in the Charlottes, this one appeared to be a place where giants played spillikins. We inspected the jumbled logs. Surprisingly, none were large enough to float the anchor. And the anchor would soon be covered by the inrushing tide.

"Damn!" said Sam, "Gotta go find a big cedar."

We all boarded *Vulture* and headed north, trailing the skiffs and glassing the shore. There were no large logs along the outer coast that suited Sam.

We rounded Cone Head and entered Rennell Sound. "That big cedar by the stream will do," Sam said, lowering the binoculars and pointing. "Just throw on a rolling hitch and stand clear."

I had done a little beachcombing with *Islander*, a tug larger than *Vulture*, and couldn't imagine that log crossing 150 feet of nasty rocks. But for once I kept my mouth shut.

George rowed while I sat in the stern holding on to the heavy salvage line. Then I stepped ashore, slipping and sliding as I dragged the line across slick, rounded rocks and between boulders. The line followed like an unwilling snake. Two spruce logs lay across the cedar. I wrapped four turns around the cedar. In theory it should roll free, but I had my doubts.

I signaled. Sam has pretty definite ideas and isn't one to bother with fine details. If wood can be made to fly, why bother to form it into an airplane or glider before launching? Sam hit the throttle. *Vulture* leaped like a happy whale. The line straightened and stretched. Without warning the log spun, bounced once or twice, and flew about twenty feet before crashing onto the rocks. The Wright brothers would have been ecstatic to have done as well at Kill Devil Hill. The log continued to flop and fly across the rocks like a wounded mallard.

"Anne, did you get that on the movie camera?" I asked after boarding *Vulture*.

"No. Too busy holding the coffeepot on the stove." She handed me a cup. "Besides, that's nothing! You should see us pull three or four logs at a time off worse beaches!"

The log dashed sideways and then alternately became submerged and leaped to the surface like a playful porpoise as we rushed full-bore back to the wreck.

We pulled the log shoreward with the skiff, helped along by the incoming waves. Retreating waves jerked it away. "Doesn't look like there'll be enough water to float it across the reef," I said as we strained on the line. Then another wave rolled and bounced it toward us a few inches.

George came ashore to help. Once more I went into the water to get a second line around the log. Pulling and hauling, we gained a few feet. "Only eight more to go," said George. Then the log hung up on a tiny projection. Was that rock pimple going to defeat us?

Sam tooted *Vulture's* whistle. It was high tide. We had to get that log in now or else wait twelve hours. Waves rolled in, irregular in size. One lifted the log; the two or three that followed only rocked it. Then a wave tumbled ashore and rolled the heavy cedar over the troublesome projection and into the crevice beside the anchor.

Immediately that stubborn log tried to ride the outflow. We slipped a third line onto the log. Betty and I braced on opposite sides of the crevice while George held on from the end, each of us hauling or slacking as wave after wave toyed with the log. This seemed to go on all afternoon, but it was actually just over two hours before the cedar made its last attempt to escape.

Sam came ashore with a small chain saw. "Won't do to wrap a boom chain around that slick log and have it slip off," Sam said. "We'd likely lose the anchor in deep water." He quickly notched the log.

Once more I jumped into the water. We worked the buoyed chains around the log and into the notches before driving toggles through the rings, connecting both ends of the chain.

"Shackle those chains together, Neil," Sam directed, producing two shackles from somewhere.

Sometime during all this, Betty noticed that the crown swiveled on the shank. Layers of thick rust had caused it to look like a solid forging. Those strange projections on the reverse side of each fluke bothered me; they were pointed in the wrong direction to be of use in catting the anchor.

While I was hopping around in the chill water, Betty said something about keeping my clothes on. As always, Sam cut right to the crux: "After a couple minutes in there *nobody* could tell if that was Angus or Agnes! So forget it."

It took fifteen minutes to secure the anchor and log together. Now the tide couldn't come in fast enough for us.

We had plenty of time for beachcombing. George found one of the masts tumbled in with a stack of drift logs. "Would have missed it but saw those four iron hoops," he said as we measured its diameter—twenty-one inches. Then we scrambled about trying to determine its length. One end was covered by logs, but what we could see was seventeen feet long. The wood was soft, its grain deteriorated.

I searched from pebbled beach to tree line, looking for any part of the ship and finding three more deadeyes, one attached to a thick chunk of oak gunwale. A massive broken section of joined timbers—probably *Florence's* overturned keel—lay at the beach's upper limits, partially covered by sand and gravel.

After scratching away the gravel and rolling off the smaller logs, I crawled under one end. The heaviest timber had been notched to receive a mast and then skillfully built up to reinforce it. Long rods, as thick as my thumb, driven through snug holes and peened over large washers, held these timbers together. Straight-grained ash treenails, their ends wedged wide, alternated with the rods.

The red summer sun was balancing on the cloudless horizon when Sam and George rowed ashore towing a salvage line. "That line cost lotsa dollars—dollars earned salvaging logs and boats, not recovering worthless old anchors," Sam said. "And I don't want it chaffed on these sharp rocks."

The temperature dropped with the sun. Already the rising tide slapped against the cedar log and covered the anchor. All I had to do was shackle the towline onto a boom chain. The log became livelier as each incoming wave sneaked under and lifted it. We had waited too long—just to save that hunk of salvage line.

I hopped aboard the bucking log. Twice Betty screamed at me to get off. She wanted that anchor but had visions of my being crushed between log and jagged basalt. Finally, the simple task of shackling was accomplished, mostly underwater by feel.

The evening high tide was only inches higher than the forenoon high. There was no chance—as I had hoped—of the anchor being lifted straight out of the crevice and floated off.

Sam moved the tug into position, maintaining a light but steady pull. For fifteen minutes *Vulture* pulled at half power, gaining a foot, sometimes two, as each incoming wave toyed with the cedar. One fluke hung down, its tip catching at every bounce.

At high tide Sam gunned the diesel. Water sprayed from every fiber of the towline. Rust accumulated during the past seventy years broke loose in an instant as the fluke swiveled up and away from the rock. Log and anchor skidded, sparked, and bounced across the ragged reef, chipping rock, grinding wood, and scaling rust. Then it leaped off the reef and into deep water.

"We made it!" Betty yelled and we laughed and shouted with joy.

Then the log and anchor sank.

Not knowing just what had happened, Betty and I ran back to our skiff and rowed to *Vulture*.

"That's an instant deadhead!" Sam screamed as we hauled alongside. "Toss your boat aboard and we'll see what we can do." Already he was increasing the RPMs.

It was after ten o'clock—dusk—and we were tired and ready to call it a day, but we had miles to go. Slowly building up speed, we moved seaward. The three-hundred-foot towline angled down at about thirty degrees. "That tow's about a hundred feet deep," Sam said. All seemed well. There had to be some iron there, or the log would float.

"Guess you can rig your lights for a submerged tow, Sam." I was thinking of a rainy dawn when I had brought a gasoline tanker into Seattle and recognized the towing lights of a tug with a submerged tow. Now I couldn't recall the arrangement of those red and white lights.

"Who'll see us out here?" Sam growled, peering at the darkening coast. "And who would know what they meant?" To further convince me, he added, "I've had those stupid weekend sailors try to cut between my tug and tow in *daytime*. Lights only confuse such idiots."

We were outside the kelp beds of Kindakun Point, enjoying our first sips of coffee and congratulating ourselves on a memorable day and a successful salvage. Abruptly *Vulture* jerked to a stop. Coffee seared our hands and soaked our clothes.

"A damned reef!" Sam snarled as he threw the clutch into neutral and the throttle to idle.

Only minutes earlier Sam was telling us how a submerged

log fills with water and loses its buoyancy. The deeper the water, the greater the pressure and the faster the loss occurs. Now we were hooked on a reef with most of Sam's expensive towline and chain fathoms below.

If Sam made one mistake, that strong line might wrap around the propeller and shaft as if it were a reel, and the powerful engine could pull us under—stern first.

Sam demonstrated his expertise as *Vulture* twisted and pulled in various directions. At times the stern sank so low that water sloshed aboard. At last we broke loose. How much of our tow did we have? Had the flukes broken? We knew only that something heavy was still down there.

Well after midnight we rounded Cadman Island in Kano Inlet. A large flock of resting sea birds noisily took off as we approached the upward-sloping sand beach of Carew Bay. Sam headed straight for shore, touched bottom, and then backed off as I hauled in the towline until we were alongside the anchor. After taking a couple of turns around the towing bitts, we charged shoreward at full speed. In the morning, anchor and log would be dry. I unshackled the towline and brought it aboard.

Sam shot *Vulture's* spotlight along the beach. Not many logs. "You and George go over there and hook onto that log. Need the rascal if we're going to make that hunk of iron float."

Ashore, with Sam's spotlight on us, we saw that the cedar was not just a big log but a limbless tree trunk, complete with roots. It was blocked by a blown-down spruce, and a small log lay across it. Moving it looked impossible, but now I had faith in *Vulture* and her crew. We made the hookup, ran clear, and waved.

Vulture's diesel opened up, and the tug leaped seaward like an Olympic sprinter. The line knifed up from the water. Nothing happened for a fraction of a second. Then the cedar abruptly began to roll, gained momentum, spun, crashed into the spruce roots, bent them, and leaped at least twelve feet into the air before bouncing onto the sand and sliding into the salt chuck. After shoving the cedar alongside the anchor, where its roots would keep it from moving, Sam took us out to *Skylark*. We were ready to drop.

In the misty morning we inspected our prize. It had not been damaged on the reef.

More boom chains and wire rope were needed. Before leaving Sandspit I had checked with the owner of a small logging company operating at the head of Givenchy Anchorage and been assured that we could have anything we needed. We sped into the vacant camp and picked up two discarded lengths of wire rope and three boom chains.

We churned back at full speed to beat the incoming tide. Suddenly Sam slammed the throttle to stop. *Vulture* nosed down and I stumbled into the radar scope. "Damned engine's overheating," Sam said, jerking up the floorboards. The impeller for the engine cooling pump had disintegrated.

Anne, the ever-efficient assistant, was there ready to hand Sam the proper tool—often before he asked for it. In ten minutes a new impeller was installed and we were underway.

"Just had this thing overhauled by the so-called experts and paid fifteen hundred dollars ...."

I had heard that before.

The tide raced in over the wide sand beach. We worked fast, bucking off the roots and broken top and lashing the logs together with the anchor between them. To Sam and Anne, this was old stuff. Betty, George, and I had to be pointed in the right direction.

When the incoming tide lapped around the logs, *Vulture* dashed away from the land, jerking the tow into the water. This time it floated.

Glowering clouds blew in from the southwest, and cat's paws scratched the dark water. Sam headed for Skidegate Narrows, hoping to get through on the flood tide.

Vulture was in Alliford Bay when we came alongside that evening. "We'll bring the anchor into Sandspit at high tide," Sam told us before we moored *Skylark* and drove home.

The next morning we walked across the road to the beach in front of our home and saw that Sam and Anne had shoved the logs and anchor ashore. All we had to do was get a crane truck and set the anchor in our yard. We were happy. It had been a successful recovery.

"Where's your anchor?" Harold Bronsch asked that afternoon when he stopped by with his camera. Harold has seen the anchor earlier, and, since he likes to tease, I figured he was trying to shake us up.

Harold wasn't joking—that brute of an anchor was gone! For seventy years it had lain unmolested on the wild shore of the west coast. Now, a few hours in Sandspit, and it was gone.

No need to call in Sherlock Homes. Fresh tracks of heavy equipment led us to the wharf. Nearby was a Timber-Jack with *Florence's* anchor lashed to its blade. Who owned it, and why had they run away with our anchor?

Betty did the detective work. A pair of log salvagers, just in from Moresby Camp, were looking for any heavy weight to anchor their bag of logs in Shingle Bay. They had spotted the anchor, marveled at their luck in finding something that had "just drifted in," and grabbed it. They were only waiting for low tide to bury it—probably forever. That evening the log salvagers sheepishly deposited the anchor in our yard.

As Sam said, "It was a lead pipe cinch."

Sam and Anne caught the next high tide through the narrows and continued their cruise around the Charlottes, visiting Puffin Cove as they beachcombed along Moresby's west coast.

We learned that the small scoops on the arms of the anchor were devices to make it dig in better, identifying it as a rare Porter patent anchor.

Summer vacation was nearly over, and George, Becky, and George II boarded the jet to return to Laguna Beach, California, where George taught and coached. Betty and I refueled and provisioned *Skylark* and then set out for the west coast and Puffin Cove. We didn't know what lay ahead, only that each day could bring some new adventure.

Epilogue

Since we first explored the Queen Charlottes in 1955, then left Southern California in 1965, over a quarter of my life has been spent here. They have been satisfying years filled with hard work and strenuous activities. During these seventeen exciting years we have seen many changes in the Queen Charlotte Islands—some for the better, some for the worse, but all inevitable. Most changes have been the result of improved transportation and communications, the world's burgeoning population, and increased demand for natural resources.

In November 1980 the modern ferry *Queen of Prince Rupert* began runs between Prince Rupert and Skidegate several times a week. Suddenly the Charlottes lost their remoteness as load after load of visitors arrived to look, camp, fish, hunt, or move in. Of course the islanders get the benefit of reduced freight rates plus convenient and inexpensive transportation to and from the mainland.

Each settlement has grown and new camps have been built, bringing the islands' population to some seventy-five hundred persons. This is not large, considering the area, but it is more than double the population of seventeen years ago. As a result, there has been a great change in the islanders relaxed *manana* lifestyle.

Cattle no longer roam the streets of Queen Charlotte City; we no longer recognize nearly everyone living here; a stranger may be in my favorite fishing spot; homes or trailers have replaced acres of large second-growth timber; deer, bear, and otters are no longer seen just outside our home in Sandspit; I may hunt deer only nine months of the year now, and it's been years since I've bagged a buck within ten minutes of leaving home; and we no longer leave our doors unlocked.

On the plus side, stores have competition, meaning lower prices and a broader selection; items are available locally that we used to order from the city; and Sandspit-based helicopters insure fast medical evacuation or immediate search-and-rescue for vessels in distress.

Man has unintentionally upset the balance of nature here, and this imbalance is perhaps more noticeable than it would be on the mainland. Because they lack natural predators on the island, animals introduced for a good purpose now exist in numbers that are harmful to the environment.

Sitka black-tailed deer, brought in as a walking meat supply, populate the islands. Wonderful, except that they especially delight in browsing on cedar seedlings. As a result, foresters prophesy a great decline in the renewal of western red cedar trees, a valuable crop.

Squirrels, introduced, some say, to chew off cones from spruce and hemlock trees, thus making it easier to gather cones for sale, probably do the least damage of any introduced animals.

Raccoons were introduced for the trappers. Then the bottom fell out of the market, and they were no longer trapped.

As the population increased, the raccoons began migrating south, and in 1980 we first saw their tracks in Puffin Cove. Raccoons prey on ground-nesting birds, grouse and waterfowl being the most noticeable victims.

Beavers were also brought in for trapping. Now they build dams in salmon streams, preventing salmon from going upstream to spawn.

Our work at Puffin Cove is often enjoyably interrupted as we watch a doe encourage her fawn to swim across the lagoon; a sow with one or two cute cubs; a marten scurrying across the drift logs; an otter or two racing along the shore before slipping into the water to dive and soon surface with a small fish; mallards, mergansers, and Canada geese swimming along the water's edge; seals torpedoing through clear salt water and then surfacing for a quick look around; and bald eagles, ravens, red-tailed hawks, sea gulls, and crows. Checking through the bird book to identify one of the smaller feathered creatures is guaranteed to slow down typing, but every bird and animal adds infinite joy and fulfillment to each stimulating day. And of course we are always happy to have a helicopter drop in with new or old friends. It's a rare day we don't have a small sack of mail to go out with them.

We loved the Charlottes as they were when we first saw them in 1955; yet we also appreciate the conveniences and services supported by a larger population, including much better transportation by air and sea. We know we can't have it both ways. There is no going back. The earth's population is literally exploding, and we must adjust to closer contact, new restrictions, less freedom—and reduced horizons.

I'm sure most of us dream of our personal Shangri-la. By giving up the security of a regular paycheck, we gained the freedom and opportunity to live a full and varied yet simple life. It is not always easy or safe, but it is a life many people only experience for a few weeks during their annual vacation.

One of our most meaningful presents for Christmas 1981

was a card from two men working at updating maps of Canada. They informed us that the names we had chosen for Blue Heron Bay and our beloved Puffin Cove were now official.

Exchanging our oceanfront home with a swimming pool in Southern California for a small cabin in the rain forest of a North Pacific island was a good trade. I am thankful we were fortunate enough to find our paradise here in the Charlottes when it was remote and little known and while we were young enough to enjoy it to the fullest.